God, Girlfriends, & Chocolate

Encouraging Stories From the Heart

Gaye Lindfors

Scripture taken from the HOLY BIBLE, NEW INTERNATIONAL VERSION®.
Copyright © 1973, 1978, 1984 International Bible Society. Used by permission of Zondervan Publishing House. All rights reserved.

The "NIV" and "New International Version" trademarks are registered in the United States patent and Trademark office by International Bible Society. Use of either trademark requires the permission of the International Bible Society.

ISBN: 978-1475209341
Significant Solutions, Inc., St. Paul, MN

Printed in the United States of America
Book design and typesetting by Stephanie Hofhenke,
String Marketing, Inc.
Cover design by Stephanie Hofhenke, String Marketing, Inc.

First Printing: April 2012

This book is dedicated to my sisters
and best girlfriends,
Julie and Lori.

Thank you for the stories.
Thank you for the laughter.
Thank you for the journey.
I love you.

Julie, Lori & Gaye

Contents

With Gratitude

This book is about stories—the chapters that shape our lives, and the characters that make the journey more interesting. It is through stories we realize our lives are more similar than they are different. It is through stories we are encouraged. It is through stories we are reminded how much God loves us.

I am grateful to the friends who breathed life into these stories...

First of all, to the Girlfriends who have shared life's journey, and chocolate, with me—thank you. It is an extraordinary compliment to be called "Friend."

Stephanie Hofhenke is one of those special Girlfriends. She is also an amazing designer, website manager, and creative marketing guru. Stephanie has partnered with me on this writing project since the day I said, "I'm going to write another book." She is a gift to my business, and a gift to my heart.

My business coach, Mark LeBlanc, helped me take my *idea* for a book and turn it into *this* book. And this is a much better book. He is my coach and my friend.

Mary MacDonell Belisle provided more than exceptional editing skills. She understood my spirit and intentions, and offered suggestions that helped me write better stories. What a joy to work with her.

It is an honor to include chapters written by my friends,

Kelsey, Julia, Donna, Shannell, Beth, and Teri. They have allowed their stories to be shared so others can benefit.

Through her best-selling books, mentoring, and a specific weekend workshop in El Paso, Texas, eleven years ago, Laurie Beth Jones has helped me discover my divine purpose—the story God has called me to write and live. I am eternally grateful for her guidance and her friendship.

My mom and dad, George and Joyce Nornes, taught me from the day I was born that God loved me. They taught me what it means to have a relationship with Jesus that is deeper than just knowing *about* Him—it's knowing *Him*. Dad died nine years ago, and I still miss him terribly—but I see his fingerprints in every area of my life. My mom continues to model what life looks like when you believe, at your very core, that God is faithful, always. I am so blessed to have been raised by these two loving parents.

My sisters, Julie and Lori, are just the most fun people I know. Oh, how I love being their sister. They teach me what it means to love unconditionally. They give me a soft place to land when the road gets a little bumpy. And they always tell me my diet is working. I love them very much.

Early in our relationship, my husband Steve taught me that my story mattered. It's his hand I want to hold as we write our life stories.

Thank you, God, for loving me just as I am. Thank you for caring about my story.

Your story matters.

With each breath you take, with each word you speak, and with each connection you make, you are writing your story. No one else can write it. Your story is one-of-a-kind… and priceless. That's why it matters.

Have you noticed how quickly you can get to know people by the stories they tell? We learn about their experiences, their loves, their disappointments. We internalize how they see the world, what's important to them, and what they dream about. By listening to the stories, we actually learn the lessons they've learned, vicariously. **And, we remember the lessons.** Why? Stories connect with our heads and with our hearts.

God speaks to us through stories. The Bible is filled with historical narratives, letters, parables, and love songs. Each one sends a message to his children about the God who loves us so very much.

In this book, I've shared some of the stories that have influenced the person I've become and the person I want to be. You will catch a glimpse of those events and people that shaped my life when you read them. Many stories describe experiences with my sisters and girlfriends. Some may make you think about your own story. I certainly hope that more than a few of them make you laugh!

To that end, I've expanded the story pool to include six girlfriends. None of us are newsmakers. Our stories aren't told because of our accomplishments. They are included in this book because we have learned valuable lessons as our lives have unfolded. We've learned that we all love chocolate, and that chocolate can soothe a child's scraped knee, and provide comfort to an adult after a bad day at work. However, there are a few other things we have in common—His Word is written in our hearts. We love Jesus. Thus, our desire is to live an authentic life of faith in a world that demands so much of us. Primarily, our stories are for an Audience of One—Jesus. But, we want to share them with you, too.

Read several of these stories at one time, or use this book as a devotional, reflecting on one each day. After most of the chapters, I've written a prayer. I invite you to pray it, asking God what you can learn from my story. Throughout the book, you will also find "doodle" pages. These are blank pages that ask you to consider more deeply something you've read—a place for you to draw, scribble, write, journal, or make a list. A space for you to write down your story.

Thank you for spending time with me. Please let me hear from you. It would be such a gift. Your story matters.

Sharing the journey with you,
Gaye

St. Paul, Minnesota
March, 2012

Right after lunch. As a third grader, this was one of my most favorite times of the day. Marlys Johnson would come into our classroom to tell us stories. She was pretty. She was really cool. She was in high school, and to our childish eye, someone with status, like a movie star.

Marlys represented our school in the story-telling division at speech contests. Our after lunch story time was her practice. She told us fables and make-believe stories, but she always made them seem real. She helped us imagine far-away places and people we'd never met. All the characters had such amazing lives, far more interesting than our own. We were always a captive and captivated audience.

I often think about the captivating stories we fashion with our lives. Our experiences, interactions, and decisions create the storyline. This storyline belongs to nobody but us. Our emotions, reactions, and spirit breathe life into the stories. Each day we craft a new page. As we move through events and the seasons of our lives, chapters are written. Some days, we appreciate our stories. Other days, we would give away our last piece of chocolate to have someone else's story. Right?

Unlike Marlys's tall tales, our stories rarely contain castles with pretty princesses and handsome princes. They unfold in northwestern Minnesota towns or sprawling metropolitan suburbs. Some of our stories are written in the office where we've just received the pink slip, or in the ICU unit, the homeless shelter, or under the covers when we just can't face another day.

These stories celebrate good days. These stories lament bad days.

Handling the good days is pretty easy. However, when an unexpected character or unanticipated event enters into the storyline, our anxiety rises. When our plotline takes a dark turn we often put on the brave smile and play "Pretend." When asked, "How are you?" we reply, "Just fine." It's a lie.

We're afraid our own stories aren't good enough, so, we embellish.

Please hear this truth. No matter what has happened to you or what will happen to you—on bad days or good—your story matters. It has significance because God created you with talents and skills and abilities that are uniquely yours, precisely for a purpose no one else can fulfill. That makes you significant.

Now, with God's help, I shall become myself.

Søren Kierkegaard

You see, your value as a human being has nothing to do with you. It is not something you earned or deserve. **You are significant because God says so.** "*I praise you because I am fearfully and wonderfully made; your works are wonderful, I know that full well.*" (Psalms 139:14) "*I [God] have loved you with an everlasting love.*" (Jeremiah: 31:3)

And, here's the remarkable reality... Since your significance is not based on anything you've done, or on who you know, (or what you do, or how much money you make), and is, instead, based **completely** on who God is, **you can never be insignificant.** Ever.

> *The maker of the stars would rather die for you than live without you .*
>
> *Max Lucado*

Max Lucado writes in his book, *Traveling Light*, "Do you feel a need for affirmation? Does your self-esteem need attention? You don't need to drop names or show off. You need only pause at the base of the cross and be reminded of this: The maker of the stars would rather die for you than live without you. And that is a fact."

Wow. Double Wow.

Remember, we never know what's going to show up on tomorrow's story pages. Life has its ups and downs. Love. Conflict. Health and disease. We win jobs, and we lose jobs. Often it is in the joy as well as the messiness that our stories are written.

One of my favorite hymns is "Amazing Grace." It's a story every believer in Christ shares. We were lost. We were found.

"Amazing grace, how sweet the sound, That saved a wretch like me! I once was lost, but now am found; Was blind, but now I see."

We are sinners saved by grace, "Easter people, living in a Good Friday world," as the author Barbara Johnson writes. We have moments of jubilation and sheer joy, and moments of despair and sheer terror.

Remember, nobody has a story like yours, Dear Friend. And, only YOU can tell, and live, your story.

Your story matters.

Dear God,

Thank you for knowing my story. Thank you for caring about my story. Please keep me from being distracted by the storylines that seek to steal my joy. Help me write my story in obedience to who you have called me to be, and what you have called me to do. Jesus, you are the great Storyteller. Thank you for guiding my pen.

Amen.

Doodle Page...

What are some of the themes in your story?
What symbols or pictures reflect those themes?

Julie, Lori, & Gaye

There is always something to laugh about.

Gaye, Julie & Lori

Living and Laughing Out Loud

A child's giggle. It's filled with amazement, wonder, and sheer delight. You listen to a baby giggle, and watch the small body tremble with excitement, and you can't help but enter into the experience by smiling back. This is a perfectly natural reaction.

Doesn't it feel good to just laugh until the tears roll down your cheeks? Until you have trouble catching your breath? Oh, what unbridled joy! I think God calls us to laugh out loud until it hurts.

One of my favorite "laugh 'til you cry" moments was with my sisters over 35 years ago. It was a Sunday afternoon. Julie, Lori, and I were sitting in the living room, telling jokes and sharing stories. Of course, it was never enough to just *tell* a story. We became *engaged* with the story. We *became the characters in the story.* Arms moved. Bodies lurched. We sat. Then stood. We shrieked. Then, whispered. We became entertainers on a stage with our favorite audience— each other. Of course, we laughed. We got to the point where we couldn't even understand what each other was saying. Words became broken bits of noise, escaping only when we could catch our breath. That made us laugh even harder. The stories were ho-hum. However, the giggles, hiccups, cries, and silent laughs? THEY WERE HILARIOUS.

[Definition of the silent laugh: Your sister is laughing so hard that she makes no noise. Her mouth is wide, the tears are streaming down her cheeks, she is folded over at the waist, and she can't breathe. Perfect.]

Julie and Lori
New lipstick colors

Jesus came to give us a life of peace, hope, and joy. *"I have come that they may have life and have it to the full,"* says John 10:10. Grab that promise! Find the joy in today, the moment that reminds you that not everyone is out to get you, and not everything is horrible. Find one thing that will move you to, at minimum, crack a smile.

If that doesn't work? Bring in the BIG GUNS…your GIRLFRIENDS.

Just recently my sisters and I realized we were way overdue for a good laugh. Life had gotten too serious. We needed a break from the daily stressors. We needed each other. So, we cleared our calendars for a Saturday evening "Girls' Night In," ordered pizza, drank our diet pop, and ate our chocolate licorice for dessert. Of course, we told stories, and we laughed and laughed, and laughed some more. It was "just what the doctor ordered."

Yes, there is darkness in our world. Sickness, sadness, and disappointments are everyday realities. Even so, I think we confuse big-deal tragedies with daily annoyances far too often. So what if the clerk at the check-out counter gets angry with you because the radio you want to purchase doesn't have a price tag attached to it. Big deal if the erratic driver cuts you off in the fast lane. The pizza delivery guy brings you anchovy instead of pepperoni. (Does anyone really eat anchovy pizza?) Let it go. There's enough life-altering trouble in the world without making a mountain out of a herring and bad manners.

> *Life is to be experienced joyfully rather than endured grudgingly.*
>
> *Luci Swindoll*

"…Life is to be experienced joyfully rather than endured grudgingly…Why do we take the minor irritations so seriously?… [We] can't distinguish between a mere inconvenience and a major catastrophe." Luci Swindoll says it so well.

Well, what's keeping you from living and laughing out loud today? Hurts? Disappointments? Worries?

> *Joy is not simply a feeling of happiness. Joy is the all-intoxicating feeling of becoming.*
>
> *Matthew Kelly*

Remember, take a moment to consciously stop what you're doing. Think about what's good in your life, focusing on all good things that God has given you. Read a funny story. Listen to an encouraging CD. Take a walk, and remember to breathe deeply. Better yet, call a girlfriend.

I've learned not to wait for the troubles to go away. Instead, I take God at His word, choosing to find space in my heart for joy. I encourage you to do the same.

Live your life to the full.

Dear Jesus,

Thank you for promising me a full life. Thank you for caring about my happiness. Would you please help me remember the things that make me smile? Would you please help me focus on the joy that awaits me, rather than the hurt and sadness I'm feeling right now? Also, Lord, please show me how I can bring joy to someone else this week. Help me focus on the needs of someone else, rather than my own. Thank you so much for offering me a full life.

Amen.

Doodle Page...

What fun-filled moments still make you smile? What people in your life are fun to be around? Why?

My niece, Julia Joy Charron (1999)
It's gonna' be one of those days...

My Mind in the Morning

"Woke up this morning with my mind... stayin' on Jesus," sings "Mississippi" Fred McDowell. Yesterday, that was true. Today, not so much.

How is it that I can wake up in the morning and my mind is already thinking about the tough part of the day ahead? Deadlines, work, pounds to shed, and the realization that there aren't enough hours to finish all the work waiting in front of me! Ooftah.

I don't understand what happens to our brains during our sleep. Sleep should be restful, right? I go to bed feeling good about the next day and enthused about the exciting projects I've planned. Still, sometime during the night, a switch flips in my brain. My subconscious focus turns to doubt, worry, and fear. How is it that our minds wake up busy before we've had time to anticipate being busy?

The Devil loves to disturb us at this point in our day, doesn't he? It ticks me off when I think about the evil grin he must have on his face and the pleasure he takes as I lift my head off the pillow, sighing over the lengthy list of the day's duties laid out in front of me.

Here's what I have to remember...
The moment, the very moment, that my mind starts to go down the path of discouragement and weariness...I need to breathe the name of Jesus.

Remember who we're reaching for when we call His name—
> Emmanuel, God with us.
> The King of Kings.
> Redeemer.
> Savior.

I love the words of the old hymn, "Day by Day and with Each Passing Moment," written by Lina Sandell Berg.

> *He whose heart is kind beyond all measure gives unto each day what He deems best.*
>
> *Lina Sandell Berg*

> "Day by day, and with each passing moment,
> Strength I find to meet my trials here;
> Trusting in my Father's wise bestowment,
> I've no cause for worry or for fear.
> He whose heart is kind beyond all measure
> Gives unto each day what he deems best,
> Lovingly its part of pain and pleasure,
> Mingling toil with peace and rest."

God knows exactly what's going through my mind as I open my heavy eyelids in those early morning hours. I find that a comforting thought.

Here's what I've learned from one too many "heavy burden" mornings:
> I can choose what I think about.
> I can choose how I focus on the day ahead.
> I can choose Jesus.
> God expects me to do that.
> It's life-changing to walk with Him.

"You will keep in perfect peace him whose mind is steadfast, because he trusts in you." (Isaiah 26:3)

Oh, Jesus,

Sometimes my mind wakes up before the rest of my body, and it starts thinking about all the negative "stuff" before I even understand what's happening. Would you please help me to immediately think of Your Name, instead? Please fill my mind with Your love and Your peace during my sleep, so that I wake refreshed and focused on You. Jesus...Jesus...Jesus...What a beautiful name. Thank you for all the power and grace and comfort that come with your name.

Amen.

Something to think about...

What names remind you of Who Jesus is? Savior...
Redeemer...Prince of Peace...

Julia Joy Charron

Julia's Prayer

By Julia Charron

My niece, Julia, wrote a prayer when she was in the second grade. Her prayer has been taped to my mom's fridge since then. It reminds me of the simple language we can use when talking to Jesus.

From the heart and the pencil of a second-grader...

Dear Lord, help me change help me meet all the kinder gardeners and give them my kindness and my love and for all my sins to be washed as white as snow and I just want to thank you for offering to forgive me and thanks for watching me and help me express my feeling on paper and help me love you and I could go longer but I can't I'll write more later.

julia

Donna Fagerstrom
Leading Worship

This is My Story, This is My Song.
By Donna Fagerstrom

"Being confident of this, that He who began a good work in you will be faithful to complete it." Philippians 1:6

I recently read a sign that said, "Home is where your story begins." My story begins at home and does not paint a pretty picture of my childhood life, so I have never shared my personal testimony out of love, honor, and respect for my parents. I never wanted people to judge them for what they did or didn't do. As a young child I knew that I was to honor and respect my parents, and I tried to do that, until the day they both died. You may ask, why are you sharing your story now? After reading Carol Kent's newest book, *Between a Rock and a Grace Place,* I thought if Carol and Gene can share from their broken "tight" spots in life, then it's time that I did the same.

Often, when I have a speaking engagement, I'll start off with something like, "I was born at an early age." People usually laugh, but the truth is, "we" were born three months premature and lived in separate incubators for four months. Yes, I am an identical twin, and it took my parents 12 years to pay off our hospital bill. When my sister and I finally weighed five pounds, we were four months old, and the hospital released us to the care of my seventeen-year-old mother and twenty-one-year-old father.

My mom was the last of thirteen children. (Six died before they reached the age of three.) My dad was fourteen-years-old when his mother died, and he became responsible for his seven-year-old sister and four-year-old-brother. My grandfather was an absentee father, while serving as a Captain of the Coast Guard. It is my parents' back story that becomes foundational for my story.

As a child, I never doubted I was loved. However, I lived in an alcoholic home with great shame and fear. My precious dad was the most loving and giving man I knew when he wasn't drinking. I lived in shame, fearful of discovery. I also lived in fear of what my dad would do when he drank too much. As a little girl, I witnessed my mom being beaten so badly that I was afraid she would not survive until morning. I lived with the shame of never being able to have friends over to our house because I never knew if my dad would be sober when I arrived home.

There are some scars that never heal. I don't ever remember a Christmas when my dad was sober. Every Christmas Eve mom would hope, believe, and expect this would be the year for a joy-filled celebration. Each year we would anxiously await dad's arrival for Christmas Eve dinner and presents only to get the infamous call, "Mrs. -- your husband is in jail with a DUI. Would you please come and pick him up?" Every Christmas, I still get that anxious knot from childhood in my stomach.

Each Sunday, my mom faithfully brought my sister and me to church. Without exception, everyone else in the church was there as a family. Not the three of us. I even felt shame at church because I was knew I was different, and I always felt people's pity. But, I'm so very grateful for my mom's courage and heart for the things of God. I will forever be in her debt.

I remember well how much my dad wanted to quit drinking. He and I went to scores of AA meetings, and he also went to the hospital on several occasions to conquer the lifelong grip alcohol had on him. (You see, my grandfather thought it was funny when he would put beer in my dad's baby bottle. Dad never stood a chance, he died alone at the age of 51.) I don't blame my parents for life's struggles.

There is so much more to the story, but let me share a vivid conversation the Lord and I had a few years ago. It was as though He was asking me, which would I choose? The home I grew up in, or the pleasant and peaceful home our daughter grew up in? I thought about it for a long while. I couldn't imagine growing up in a home where there was no fighting, yelling, screaming, beatings, or alcohol abuse. In the end, I told the Lord I would choose the home I grew up in, because it shaped me into the person I am today. (To be honest, I still wrestle from time to time with the fear and shame of someone's judgment if they become aware of my home background.)

> *Life is tough but God is faithful.*
>
> *Sheila Walsh*

On numerous occasions, I've had people share with me how wonderful it must be to have had such a perfect life. (Obviously, they know little of my past.) Yes, God has been good. When I invited Him into my life at age six, I pressed forward. I threw myself into school, music lessons, Youth for Christ, and the church. I met a wonderful young man at Youth for Christ who became my husband several years later. Having a call placed on my life for full-time ministry, we have had the privilege, along with our wonderful daughter, to serve the Lord in four churches, one Seminary, and now, in our present position at Converge Worldwide. My story can be summed up in these lyrics by gospel singer and song writer, André Crouch:

Through it All

I've had many tears and sorrows, I've had questions for tomorrow. There've been times I didn't know right from wrong. But in ev'ry situation, God gave blessed consolation that my trials come to only make me strong.

I thank God for the mountains. And I thank Him for the valleys, I thank Him for the storms He brought me through. For if I'd never had a problem, I wouldn't know that He could solve them, I'd never know what faith in God could do.

Through it all, through it all, Oh, I've learned to trust in Jesus, I've learned to trust in God. Through it all, through it all, I've learned to depend upon His Word.

We can allow the choices of others to cripple us or to give us the confidence to push through. We can allow our trials to make us bitter or better. We choose.

Doug and Donna Fagerstrom

Abba,

Thank you that you are always with me, even during those times of hiding for fear of being beaten. Thank you that you allowed those hard, difficult times of fear and shame to give me a heart that cares about people who are hurting. Thank you that you are the Healer, Gentle Shepherd, and the Almighty God. Thank you that I've learned to depend upon your Word. Thank you that you began a good work in me, and you will be faithful to complete it.

In Your Precious Name,

Amen.

Gaye & Laurie Beth Jones

Living My Life with Purpose

On September 15, 2002, I decided to quit my job as Director of Human Resources for Northwest Airlines / Delta. I wrote in my journal on that day, "I have decided to resign. So much joy. Complete peace. I don't have another job yet—God has something in store for me."

Five weeks later I was a very joy-filled, re-energized, unemployed, middle-aged woman, beginning the journey toward living the life she was meant to live. I said good-bye to a great group of colleagues and friends, and Significant Solutions, Inc. opened for business.

I left behind a corporate career that had focused a great deal on organizational objectives, personal goals, and moving up the promotional ladder. Like many of my colleagues and friends, success had been defined by title, perks, salary, and location of my box on the organization chart. By those definitions, I had been doing quite well. My career and accomplishments had been very rewarding, and I'd been advising a business unit of 11,000 employees for an international Fortune 500 company.

I had enjoyed working in corporate America. The synergy with colleagues, engaging conversations with smart people, and amazing opportunities to build on my skills and experiences challenged and energized me. But, my heart had longed to commit to something else. I hadn't known what that "something else" would be; I had simply known that I needed a reason for living that was bigger than my job.

I had spent countless hours studying, praying, reading, and engaging my friends and family in discussions on finding my purpose, calling, or mission, creating my life vision, and how to live more intentionally. The pivotal experience in that journey was when I attended a workshop facilitated by Laurie Beth Jones, best-selling author of *The Path: Creating Your Mission Statement for Work and for Life.* During that weekend workshop, I realized God had put me on this earth for a specific purpose. Core values, passions, skills, and the vision I had for my life paved the way for identifying the person I was called to be and what I was called to do. My life's purpose became clear—to highlight, celebrate, and inspire significance in myself and others. As my deeply-rooted core value, significance became my stake in the ground. My work, my volunteer activities, and my relationships needed to demonstrate or affirm the significance of each individual.

> *You are either living your mission, or you are living someone else's. Which shall it be?*
>
> *Laurie Beth Jones*

That brings my story back to that Friday morning in September, 2002. While listening to a discussion during a senior leadership team meeting, I realized there was very little conversation that was inspiring a sense of significance for any of us. This isn't a criticism of the team; it's just that the gap between the corporation's purpose and my purpose was so great. Our values were not aligned. I heard myself softly whisper under my breath, "It's time to go." I was right. I have never looked back.

Our deepest calling is to grow into our own authentic selfhood, whether or not it conforms to some image of who we ought to be.

Parker Palmer

What has God called you to do? What values matter most to you? How do you want to live your life? Don't wait for your purpose to simply appear. Discover it. Ask questions. Dig deep into your heart and soul and find what really matters. Pick up a copy of Laurie Beth's book and study it. Call me—I'll help you!

The writer, teacher, and activist Parker Palmer wrote a book called *Let Your Life Speak*. This little book has a powerful message. One of the chapters is titled, "Now I Become Myself." Oh, what freedom, what joy is expressed in those words.

You were created with a personality, skills, and abilities that are uniquely yours by an Almighty, All-knowing God. No one else can be you. You have a purpose no one else can fulfill. No one else can write your story. That makes you divinely significant. Your life matters.

"For I know the plans I have for you,' declares the Lord, 'plans to prosper you and not to harm you, plans

to give you hope and a future. Then you will call upon me and come and pray to me, and I will listen to you. You will seek me and find me when you seek me with all your heart.'" (Jeremiah 29:11-13)

Ask God to show you where He wants you to leave fingerprints. He delights in revealing to you the path he has prepared for you. He longs to walk with you as you intentionally live out His purpose for you on this earth. Ask. He will show you the way.

Dear God,

Thank you for giving me a reason to live. Thank you for wanting to show me what you want me to do and where you want me to go. Please open my eyes to see your path. Open my ears to hear your advice. And, open my heart to accept your calling. Thank you for having a plan just for me.

Amen.

Doodle Page...

Discover your purpose...
What values matter most to you?
What do you think your God given talents / gifts are?

Lori, Julie, & Gaye

Practicing our Miss America smiles.

Miss America

As little girls, my sisters and I loved watching the Miss America pageant. We'd pick out our favorite gowns, use our homemade score cards to judge the talent competitions, and cry when Bert Parks would sing, "There She Is, Miss America." (If you don't remember Bert Parks, my apologies. Parks was emcee for the pageant from 1955-1979.) We dreamed of the day when we would look like, act like, and *be* Miss America.

We still enjoy the tradition of experiencing the pageant together. As the contestants parade across the stage, we text our opinions and call each other with our "Yeah, really?" comments during the commercials. But admittedly, our attitudes are a bit different. Now, we're looking at women who are at least 30 years younger than we are. All the dreaming in the world won't help us look like that. So of course, we resort to petty jealousies.

When we are discussing the inappropriateness of how much the slit of the dress reveals a contestant's leg, we are really saying, "I would give anything if my legs were toned and my thighs didn't jiggle." When we are appalled by how much cleavage is showing because of the low

It's never too late to be what you might have been.

George Eliot

cut evening gowns, we are really saying, "What do I need to do to keep my breasts from hanging to my waist?" When we are evaluating the four-octave vocal solos, precision ballet pirouettes, and concert level piano concertos, we are really saying, "Unbelievable, and they're smart too."

Here's what I've been reminded of as I watch, dream, evaluate, and face reality: A young woman doesn't wake up one day and decide she'll just show up that evening at the convention center and make a run for the crown. No, she makes a long-term commitment to do whatever is necessary to reach her goal. She wakes up every morning, determined to make the choices and live a life that reflects whom she wants to be.

What else does it take to succeed? Guts. I mean, really. How many of us are willing to parade around in a swimsuit on national TV? Count me out. I won't even do it at home.

My dream of being 5'10" and weighing 112 pounds evaporated years ago. My desire to be Miss America is history. However, I *do* desire to be the Gaye Lindfors God has called me to be. I need to discover what that means and

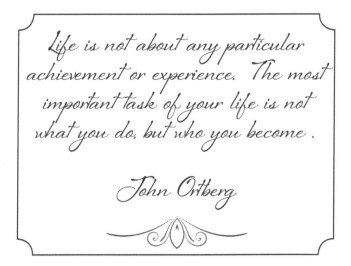

Life is not about any particular achievement or experience. The most important task of your life is not what you do, but who you become.

John Ortberg

how she looks, and commit to becoming that person, living in obedience to the teachings that will get me there.

God has put me on this earth for a purpose. I am expected to use my skills, abilities, and uniqueness to live this purpose at work, in my home, in my church, and where I volunteer. He has asked me to know Him, which means that I spend time reading his letters to me, talking with Him, and listening for his voice. He has asked me to live fully, meaning I must set aside the whining, jealousy, selfishness, and unforgiveness.

Most of us will never wear a tiara, but all of us have been offered the crown of life. *"Everyone who competes in the games goes into strict training. They do it to get a crown that will not last; but we do it to get a crown that will last forever."* (I Corinthians 9:25)

Just as it is with the accomplished, smart women who compete in the Miss America pageant, being the person God calls me to be requires that I make choices each day that support and affirm my calling and my commitment. Who has God called you to be? What are you doing today to authentically be that person?

"And, we pray this in order that you may live a life worthy of the Lord and may please him in every way—bearing fruit in every good work, growing in the knowledge of God, being strengthened with all power according to his glorious might so that you may have great endurance and patience, and joyfully giving thanks to the father, who has qualified you to share in the inheritance of the saints in the kingdom of light." (Colossians 1:10)

Thank you, God,

For creating a special place in this world, just for me. Please give me the patience and discernment I need to hear your call on my life. Please make your plans for me clear, and give me the strength and perseverance to follow your lead.

Thanks so much for loving me, just as I am.

Amen.

Doodle Page...

Who has God called you to be?
What has God called you to do?

Beth Kothe
Singing about Jesus again.

A Time to Sing

By Beth Kothe

When I was a child, my Aunt De wasn't my favorite aunt. She was prim and proper—and somewhat disapproving of this tomboy. As I became a teen, I gained new appreciation for Aunt De, a military wife who organized Bible studies from Hawaii to Morocco to New York. Anyone was welcome because she wanted everyone to know Jesus. Aunt De spent hours each day in study and prayer, talking and listening to God. When I went through a rough time as an adult, she called to let me know that she was praying for me every day. She wanted to make sure her wayward niece hadn't forgotten about God.

A few years later, Aunt De died, suddenly, in an auto accident. She had carefully pre-planned with her pastor the details of her funeral. It was her last chance to tell people about Jesus, so she carefully selected the Bible verses to be read and the hymns to be sung. She even picked the soloist—me.

It had been twenty years since I had sung in public, so I didn't know what to say when Uncle Les called. Yet, how could I deny Aunt De her last request of me? A few days later I stood in a hot, humid, little Lutheran church in Meridian, Miss., singing "What a Friend We Have in Jesus." As I returned to my seat in the pew next to my dad, he looked at me with tears in his eyes and said, "You need to start singing for Jesus again, Bethie." I promised God on the flight home that I would start singing when He showed me it was time.

> *How wonderful it is that nobody need wait a single moment before starting to improve the world.*
>
> *Anne Frank*

At the time, I was what some call a "pew Christian." I attended church most Sundays, but otherwise I wasn't involved in any way. After returning home, I got busy with life and forgot about my promise. Of course, God doesn't forget promises. Six months later I saw a note in the church bulletin that a female vocalist was needed for the praise band. Even I couldn't miss that sign. I made an appointment to audition immediately after that service so I wouldn't chicken out. I passed the audition, and suddenly, was singing about Jesus again. I was also hanging out with more mature Christians who challenged and encouraged me to deepen my relationship with Jesus. My life is richer today because my dear, sweet aunt remembered my voice and reminded me why I sing.

James, one of Jesus' brothers wrote, *"It isn't enough just to have faith. Faith that doesn't show itself by good deeds is no faith at all—it is dead and useless."* (James 2:17 NLT)

Aunt De put her faith into action in her study groups, her personal practices and her plan for her funeral. Because of her, I now put my faith into action, too. What do your actions say about your faith? What will your legacy of faith be after you leave this earth?

God,

My time is so full with all that I have to do. Show me what work you have planned for me to do. Draw me to your Word, and show me your will for my life. Thank You for those who come to you in prayer for me. Help me to be faithful in prayer for those I love.

Amen.

Kelsey Joy Charron
A Heart for God

A Whole in My Heart
By Kelsey Charron

My niece, Kelsey, has a heart that loves God. As a young girl, she discovered the "wholeness" that comes only from knowing Jesus.

From the heart and the pen of a teenager...

There is a whole in my heart that didn't used to be.
Love, joy, and peace burst inside a me.
It happened that day when I looked upon the cross,
Gazed at my reflection and saw that I was lost.
"Lord Jesus, save me!" I cried out through the dark,
And after those few words, I felt a little spark.
Who knew a short sentence could make such a change,
Could make happiness grow, and expand love's range.
Who knew small words could change spark into fire,
And bring hope to situations that seem completely dire.
God sent His Son to forgive and save me,
And there's a whole in my heart for
He has forever changed me.

Lynette Joy
(1956)

Mom, Dad,
David,
Julie & Gaye
(1960)

Mom, Dad, Lori, Julie, Gaye
(1965)

Our Family

Our lives are shaped by stories. Sometimes, the stories written by the lives of others have the greatest impact.

My parents had seven children. Yet, only Julie and Lori and I grew up together. Mom's and dad's unshakable trust in God during those sad times after the deaths of my sister and three brothers had a profound influence on my understanding of faith.

My older sister, Lynette, died just three months before I was born. I wish I could have met her—in our baby pictures, we look almost identical. My twin brothers, David and Danny, were born between Julie and Lori, and died when they were very young. Another brother didn't survive mom's pregnancy. He was going to be named Kevin.

It was through their lives and deaths that mom and dad taught me a most important lesson, one that now frames my view of the world: God is faithful. Always.

When my parents' grief was the greatest, I never heard them ask "Why?" They never complained. They didn't give up. They just kept praying. What a marvelous gift for a young child to observe.

Many years ago my dad wrote down his thoughts about losing Lynnette and the twins. His stories weren't intended to be written for publication, or serve as biographies of their lives. They haven't been edited for better reading. He simply wrote his thoughts and his recollections about those tough days. They're simply...his stories. My mom's words are part of the stories she has told us for over fifty years. Her message never changes: God is faithful. Always.

Lynette

In my dad's words...

A beautiful baby. A picture of health. And then one day she fainted—she became almost stiff. What was wrong? An appointment with the local doctor and then a heart specialist revealed a heart with a hole in it. Our little Lynette Joy had a rare congenital heart defect called "Tetralogy of Fallot." The doctors told us to go home and give her the same love and kindness we had already been giving her.

Trying months followed—a particular burden for Joyce who was home doing most of the caring. We had an oxygen tank with us all the time in case Lynette stopped breathing. On some days, we had to use it many, many times. The doctors said an operation would soon be possible. We waited.

Lynette's condition worsened and finally, the decision was made to operate. She was 2½ years old. Her chance of surviving the surgery was 50-50. The night before the operation we said goodbye, not knowing if we would see her again. We went outside the hospital and looked up at the third-floor window for a long time, not saying a word, silently praying. Then, we reminisced about the trip down and how Lynette had learned to drink a malt through a straw. We discussed her chances and outwardly talked very positively about them. But I knew within.

We didn't sleep well, and the next day it was a long wait in the parents' room. Over thirteen hours. Then, the word came. The operation was a success. Later we were able to visit her. She lay in a cold oxygen chamber, only accessible to us through a hole where we could touch her arm. She wanted her arm untied.

Later we were told we could go home. Everything was positive, her doctor said. He would call us if there was a change. At 3:00 a.m. we got the call. She had taken a turn for the worse. "How soon can you be here?" Twenty minutes. We were silent most of the time, because I know I expected the worst. I had to be brave. I did not cry.

We arrived at the hospital. The doctor said she had passed away. She had not withstood the shock of the surgery. I cried and comforted Joyce. The trip home was long and tearful. The gnawing feeling of "What else could we have done?" still lingered. Only God knows.

David and Danny

In my dad's words...

Twin boys. Oh, boy, oh, boy! What a joyful day. David George and Daniel George were a little premature and incubators were needed.

Days passed and then, weeks. The boys were still in the hospital. "A little while longer," the doctor said. We knew something was wrong. Finally, we told the doctor, "Tomorrow, we are going to talk about the twins." He agreed. He said David and Danny were macrocephalic. [The circumference of their heads was greater than the average child's.] And they were blind, deaf, and mentally retarded. He advised us not to take them home.

Time passed, but not the inner ache. Seven months later, our smallest boy, Danny, passed away. Even though we had never had him home, we loved him very much. I cried. I was not resentful or bitter, just lonely.

Several years later, Joyce and the girls and I were in Seattle for a National Education Convention. David was 4½ years old. An emergency call came for us. My father told me that David had passed away. I did not cry. I found Joyce and the girls at the park. I told them that David had died. They cried. I kept my cool until after the funeral. I went into the church basement for the fellowship with relatives and friends. I cried uncontrollably. No bitterness, only a severe inner hurt that still lingers.

I am very thankful to God for a wife and three lovely daughters, and for the months and years that he'd given us to love three other children as well. It will be a glorious day to see our beloved Lynette, David, and Danny in heaven, "where there is no more sickness or sorrow!"

Our Children

In my mom's words...

I have had a very blessed life. The only thing that I wish would have been different was to have had all our children survive.

I remember driving home from the hospital after Lynette died. George stopped to fill gas on the car. Lynette's sweater was on the front seat between us, and I picked it up and held it to my face, breathing in her sweet smell. The grief was overwhelming. Almost too much to bear. But I knew God would get me through this.

David and Danny stayed in the hospital—they were so sick. We would take Gaye and Julie with us to visit them. They'd reach their tiny arms through the crib railings, and we'd say a prayer at the end of each visit. I remember the weekend we were able to take David out of the hospital for a few days. It was so nice to be together as a family.

I was very sad when my children died. But I never believed that God was being mean to me. The Lord took good care of them when they were living, even though they were each very sick. I am so grateful for the time they were with us.

I think I learned a lot about being a teacher from having children who were so sick. When one of my grade school students felt pain or unhappiness, I really cared about how they were feeling. I always looked for the good parts of each student, even when their parents didn't think the child was good enough.

God was very faithful when our children died. Our family and friends helped us so much. I waited on the Lord. He gave me calmness. I knew that this was God's will.

God is always good and kind. He is always faithful.

Trust in the Lord with all
your heart and lean not on
your own understanding; in
all your ways acknowledge
him, and he will make your
paths straight.
Proverbs 3:5-6

God's Strength
A Place to Relax

An untroubled mother carried her young daughter down the sidewalk as I watched. The little girl's legs were wrapped around her mother's waist; pink leggings and white tennis shoes dangling in complete relaxation from her mother's hips. Her tiny, soft arm curled around her mother's neck as her dimpled chin rested on the strong shoulder of the attentive woman who had carried her since conception.

It was a perfect picture of strength and serenity.
I want someone to carry *me* like that. (I *need* someone to carry me like that.)

Today it would feel liberating to not be in charge, to not be the decision-maker. I want someone else—someone strong—to carry me.

It would feel so freeing to relax…to let go as completely as a child.

Dear Lord,
Would you carry me for a little while?
Would you let me just dangle my feet and breathe deeply while I find strength in your arms? Thank you.

Doodle Page...

What burdens do you want God to carry for you today?
Ask Him – he will take them.

Shannell McMillan

Shannell & Gaye

The Intolerable Compliment
By Shannell McMillan

At a very early age, I recall being very afraid and associating it with weakness. I remember uncontrollably crying my first day of kindergarten and being consoled with the words, "Don't cry, you're a big, **strong** girl."

In the first grade, my teacher died of a heart attack, and again the fear and sadness welled up inside of me. As the tears flowed, I was assured she was in a better place and told "you are **stronger** than this."

In the third grade, I lost my favorite aunt to Leukemia. She died 40 days from diagnosis, and in my pain and sorrow I was once again assured that she was "in a better place" and encouraged to remember I was "**stronger** than this, a tough cookie."

My ideals were being formed, and I was beginning to write the script of my life. I came to believe I was **stronger** than fear, death, sadness, and disappointment. When I came to know the Lord, His overwhelming love would envelop me, my tears would

> *My grace is sufficient for you, for my power is made perfect in weakness.*
>
> *2 Corinthians 12:9*

flow without reason, and I would stop the crying, telling myself "you are *stronger* than this."

Even though these feelings brought great peace and relief, there were other overwhelming emotions hiding inside of me threatening to surface. In a panic, I would shove those emotions away, all of them. Thus, I lived in a world of emotional isolation—a world I had created where not to feel was safe, and where "being strong" meant being emotionless and in control at all times. At times, I could hear the Lord calling me to Himself, but the fear of the unknown and the emotions it evoked were the fear that kept Him at bay and me from knowing true fellowship with my Abba Father.

One day as I was studying Paul, I read his words, "When I am weak, He is strong." I stared in disbelief at those words on the page. I felt the Lord talking directly to my heart. Tears welled up inside, and a warm blanket of love enveloped me. The years of emotion I had locked down in my attempt to "be strong" poured forth in waves of relief as the Lord comforted me. No longer do I feel the need to deny myself my emotions, or "judge" them as weakness.

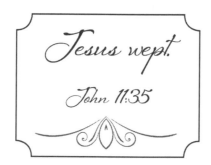

Jesus wept.

John 11:35

The Lord has since surrounded me with people who celebrate my vulnerability, remind me of His strength, and care enough not to give me the now intolerable compliment.

Dear Papa God,

Thank you for creating me perfect in my imperfections. I pray over all the women who, for years, feel the real burden to be strong for the sake of their families, their children, or in their circumstances when what they really feel is vulnerable and unsure. I thank you that I can come to the very throne room of grace in my time of great need and receive your love and your grace. Your Word calls me to cast the whole of my care upon you so that You can do the caring for me, allowing me to rest, refresh, and trust in you. Thank you for reminding me that, when I am weak, you are strong.

Amen.

Something to think about...

What emotions are you afraid to let go of, or work through? Forgiveness, anger, bitterness?

How would it feel if you didn't cling to them anymore?

Life is the
sum of
all your
choices.

Albert Camus

The Morning Wake-Up Call

Now is the moment of decision.

The time is 5:00 a.m. I'm in a beautiful state of relaxation, cozy warm under the covers. My breathing is steady and slow. Every muscle has finally decided to relax. However, now it's time to get up.

This is where the day begins for all of us: in the making of a decision. Do I keep the commitment I made to myself about getting out of bed so there's time for devotions, exercise, and finishing my oatmeal? Or, do I give in to the bliss of slumber and then, go crazy during the two-minute "getting ready" drill before my first appointment? This is **NOT** an easy choice.

I was reminded this morning about where a decision begins. It originates in my head and will.

Last night I carefully planned today's schedule. I would get up early to finish some writing on this book before going to the YMCA. I'd be able to get home after working out, do my devotions, and eat a healthy breakfast before mom's medical appointment. It would be a tightly-scheduled day, and getting everything done would hinge on keeping my commitment to get out of bed when the alarm sounded.

Now, I can talk myself into or out of *anything* if I take the time to have the conversation. The trick about keeping that early morning commitment was not to engage in the chit-chat. Unfortunately, this morning the chit-chat conversation took on a life of its own.

Actually, I was awake before the alarm radio began sharing news from around the world. However, I was still tired. So, I facilitated a lengthy discussion with myself about the virtues of getting more sleep. If I would rest for an extra five minutes, I'd be more refreshed, my writing would improve, and there would still be time to get everything done if I shaved a few minutes off my treadmill commitment. And, I could read a short Psalm instead of something from both the Old and New Testaments. Well, the five minutes of "extra sleep" turned into ten, then fifteen minutes of half-sleep with worries about "fitting in" *any* devotions before I had to jump into the car. I woke up with a start, realizing it was now going to be tough getting to mom's appointment on time.

And, the other consequences of indulging in the morning chit-chat? The writing didn't get done. The exercising didn't get done. The devotions didn't get done. Breakfast was a Diet Pepsi. And I felt **AWFUL**.

Here's the deal...
When you have those early morning chit-chats with yourself, you will always lose. Usually, nothing good comes from them.

So keep the conversation from beginning. Just get up. When the clock tells you it's "commitment time," don't even think about it. Just throw the covers back, put your feet on the floor, take a deep breath, and standup. There. You've kept your first commitment of the day. The rest of the day will thank you.

If you're looking for all the reasons why decision and follow-through is such a big deal, read Rory Vaden's exceptional book, *Take the Stairs*. This quote is a great reminder of what we probably know, but have chosen to forget: "Successful people have the self-discipline to do things they don't want to do. They do the things they don't want to do even when they don't feel like doing them."

I have a love-hate relationship with getting out of bed in the morning. The two choices I face—getting up or staying in bed—offer me two positives—accomplishments and sleep. The big question is, which choice gets me closer to living my dream life? Devotions, exercise, and oatmeal are usually the right answer.

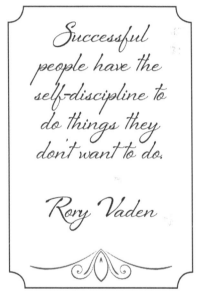

Successful people have the self-discipline to do things they don't want to do.

Rory Vaden

The disciples encountered a moment of choice and commitment in the Garden of Gethsemane. Jesus was overwhelmed with sorrow. He knew that his death was moments away, and He asked the disciples to keep watch with him. What did they do? They fell asleep. (The act of falling asleep when Jesus has asked me to watch with Him seems incomprehensible. Then, I remember all those early mornings when I'm sitting in my chair, Bible open on my lap, a notebook at my side, and I'm snoring. The notion of falling asleep, even after the request of the Master, doesn't seem so farfetched.) Jesus said, *"Could you men not keep watch with me for one hour? Watch and pray so that you will not fall into temptation. The spirit is willing, but the body is weak."* Ouch. Those words sting with truth.

Keeping my commitments—beginning with my response to the morning wake-up call—significantly influences how I feel about myself and my work. Each time I choose to keep a commitment, I strengthen my resolve and ability to move in the direction of my dreams. Viktor Frankel said it so well, "Man does not simply exist, but always decides what his existence will be, what he will become in the next moment." Each choice we make, each decision we carry-out, creates our future.

Which of your commitments have become too easily broken? What chit-chat conversations have become overly frequent? If you bundle all the decisions you make today— what you eat, where you go, what you say, how you act— what is the result? Did you live today, creating the life you have been called to live? Or, did you take the easy way out, choosing to create a ho-hum life, filled with disappointments and broken promises.

What matters most to you? Make the decision to honor **what matters most.**

Lord Jesus,

Would you please help me keep my priorities straight? Please stop the chit-chat in my head when the alarm goes off.

Help me to stay focused on the day in front of me. Thank you for showing me the choices you want me to make. Thank you for giving me enough hours in the day to accomplish what is most important—when I stay focused. Thank you, Jesus, for caring about my taking responsibility for my commitments.

Amen.

My Mom, Joyce Nornes

"Trust in the Lord with all your heart, and do not lean on your own understanding. In all your ways acknowledge him, and he will make straight your paths."
Proverbs 3:5-6

Guard Your Heart

Our hearts. We know we can't live without them, and there are times when it's difficult to live with them!

My mom's heart has beaten erratically for years. At times, it gallops towards the finish line, and at other times, it has trouble exiting the starting gate. Mom can always tell when it's irregular—her erratic pulse, lack of energy, and chest palpitations are all good indicators that her heart is operating like a roller coaster.

A few years ago she was fitted for a pacemaker and defibrillator. This mechanical device, with leads that make the connections with her heart, is located just under her collarbone. Now, it regulates her heart rhythm. It should extend her life expectancy, a very good thing. (And, simply amazing!)

A person has a lot of time to think, sitting in clinics and hospital rooms. And, during one of those waiting room visits, I thought about

> *Above all else, guard your heart, for it is the wellspring of life.*
>
> *Proverbs 4:23*

my own heart. Physically, it may beat regularly, but are there symptoms indicating it's not as healthy as it should be? (Please note that I'm not talking about cholesterol levels or clogged arteries.) We know when our heart isn't working as it should, the symptoms cannot be ignored.

"What comes out of a man is what makes him 'unclean.' For from within, out of men's hearts, come evil thoughts, sexual immorality, theft, murder, adultery, greed, malice, deceit, lewdness, envy, slander, arrogance, and folly. All these evils come from inside and make a man 'unclean.'" (Mark 7:20-23)

That's a pretty explicit list of things not to do. It's easy to rationalize, "Of course I'm not involved in *those* things!" Then, I'm reminded of what King David said to his son Solomon: *"And you, my son Solomon, acknowledge the God of your father, and serve him with whole-hearted devotion and with a willing mind, for the Lord searches every heart and understands every motive behind the thoughts."* (I Chronicles 28:9)

> *There is nothing I can hide from God. He searches my heart and understands every motive.*

Now, that Biblical passage really feels personal, doesn't it? There's not much I can hide from God! He searches my heart and understands every one of my motives. Wow. (BIG Wow.)

I started musing about these modern day miracles and technologies able to "fix" something as delicate and complicated as a heart.

It seemed as though the path to getting mom's heart rhythm regulated was the same path available to do a thorough review of my heart—from God's perspective.

The four steps the doctors followed to control mom's heart rhythm included:
1. Evaluate the symptoms.
2. Make a diagnosis.
3. Develop a course of treatment.
4. Follow-up.

Using those same four steps, here's what I did to fix my spiritual heart:

1. **Evaluate the symptoms.**

I asked myself these questions:

What am I like to be around? Am I flourishing or floundering? What words come out of my mouth? What actions speak louder than my words? Am I caring? Impatient?

Without sharing the details, let me just say that it didn't take an M.D. to bring my symptoms to my attention. They were very apparent once I became *intentionally aware* of my own behaviors.

2. **Make a diagnosis.**

"As water reflects a face, so a man's heart reflects the man." (Proverbs 27:19) I diagnosed my heart wasn't "beating" right. It wasn't healthy. Neither a pacemaker nor a defibrillator was the answer. I needed to see my sin for what it was— disobedience to God's Word. Once we confess what we're dealing with, we can figure out the appropriate steps to turn things around.

3. **Develop a course of treatment.**

My heart needed more than a tune-up or mechanical device. It needed a complete overhaul. I needed to get rid of the junk that was at the core of my heart, and let God create a pure heart within me. *"Create in me a pure heart, O God, and renew a steadfast spirit within me. Do not cast me from your presence or take your Holy Spirit from me. Restore to me the joy of your salvation and grant me a willing spirit, to sustain me."* (Psalm 51:10-12)

4. **Follow-up.**

Repentance, forgiveness, and acceptance of God's love—it comes down to choices we make. Just as my mom needs her mechanical device to keep her heart beating regularly, I need to think, talk, and act in ways that align with what God teaches us. Consistently.

Our hearts keep no secrets. When my mom's physical heart isn't working right, we know it. We see the symptoms in her daily living. The same thing is true for my heart. When it's not healthy, the symptoms show up in my daily living through my actions, attitudes, and words. So what has been my big lesson in all this? I must guard my heart at all costs.

I need to take care of my heart physically—eat right, exercise, and cut back on (notice I didn't say "eliminate") the M&Ms. Also, I need to care for the very core of my spiritual heart—nourish it by reading God's Word, protect it through prayer, and strengthen it by making smart choices. In the same way my mom depends on her mechanical device, I must depend on the Bible and God's voice.

"Above all else, guard your heart, for it is the wellspring of life." (Proverbs 4:23)

Dear God,

It doesn't always feel good to be reminded that you know exactly what's going on in my heart all the time. And yet, there is a sense of freedom and relief knowing that you still love me, even when my heart is sinful. Thank you for gently and not-so-gently nudging me when my heart isn't healthy. Please help me to be mindful of the symptoms that tell me it's time to check things out, seek forgiveness, and get back on track. Thank you for your unconditional love for me in my weakness.

Amen.

Something to think about...

How is your heart?

1. Evaluate the symptoms.

2. Make a diagnosis.

3. Develop a course of treatment.

4. Follow-up.

Girlfriends
(1963)

The glory of friendship is not the outstretched hand, nor the kindly smile, nor the joy of companionship: it is the spiritual inspiration that comes to one when he discovers that someone else believes in him and is willing to trust him.

Ralph Waldo Emerson

Girlfriends

I grew up in Climax, Minn., a small farming community in the northwest corner of the state—population 310—until more people moved out of town. My friend, Denae, lived across the Red River on a farm in North Dakota.

Denae was fun, sarcastic, smart, witty, caring, and fun. (Did I say fun?) I loved staying overnight at her house. She had sisters, too. I would study her older sister as she got ready for a date—observing and learning how to put on the eyeliner, talking about what to wear, and asking all kinds of questions about boys. Denae and I would laugh with her younger sisters as we'd dramatically entertain each other with stories and opinions about our teachers, classmates, and crushes. Her parents, Arlen and JoAnn, would chuckle and shake their heads at our shenanigans, and we'd roll our eyes as they played Eddy Arnold records on the phonograph.

In addition to an extraordinary friendship of loyalty, Denae gave me two other special gifts. The first

> *All I really need is love, but a little chocolate now and then doesn't hurt!*
>
> *Lucy Van Pelt*

Denae

gift was a genuine act of kindness. In our junior year, I didn't have a date for the prom. (And, almost *everybody* went with *somebody*. I mean, really. There were only 28 kids in our class.) Denae sensed my awkwardness and "just let me die now" emotions when it was time to take prom pictures. She let me take my prom picture with her and her boyfriend. That picture makes us laugh now. Back then? It was an act of compassion and grace.

Denae's second gift was a scarf. And it was not just any ordinary scarf. She knit this one herself. She and her parents and four sisters had taken a road trip to California. Denae knit all the way there and all the way back. (As she describes it, "Seven people packed into a sedan, five sisters in a car for that many days, and you need needles in your hands for protection!") I wore a purple winter coat at the time, and Denae knit me a multicolored purple scarf. She said they had only traveled

Gaye

from North Dakota to California and back. I think they must have traveled across the entire country *three times* because the scarf was about 17 feet long! I could wear it as a turban, a neck scarf, and an attractive body wrap that reached to my ankles. It was beautiful.

Denae and I and our other female classmates at Climax School shared a lot of tears and cheers during our school years. They were great friends to grow up with. Since then, new girlfriends continue to appear in my life's story. We laugh, cry, celebrate, and eat chocolate together.

Speaking of chocolate…throughout the years, M&Ms have usually been my chocolate of choice when planning a girls' get-together. (You add them to the top of a scoop of ice cream with Hershey's chocolate syrup, and, oh my word, it's a feast!) If only someone could find a way to remove the calories.

What a tremendous responsibility it is to be a friend. What a tremendous gift it is to have a friend.

God, girlfriends, and chocolate. Enough said.

Dear God,

Thank you for the beautiful gift of friendship. Thank you especially for my girlfriends, those friends who know what to say at just the right times. Please help me be the kind of friend that reflects your love. Show me who needs a word or a smile today. Show me who needs a friend. And Jesus, thank you for being my best friend.

Amen.

Beth Kothe

She did not show up as raw material to be shaped into whatever image the world might want her to take. She arrived with her own gifted form, with the shape of her own sacred soul. Biblical faith calls it the image of God in which we are all created.

Parker Palmer

Mistaken

By Beth Kothe

Wife. Mother. Sister. Daughter. Friend. We each have words that describe who we are. I once read that the first word that comes to your mind is the one that most defines you. My word for the first half of my life was a hard one—mistake. I was raised in a loving family. My mother used to say that our family was special because God went to extra trouble to put us together. You see, my brother, sister, and I were each adopted by my parents, who were unable to conceive. I was adopted as an infant in 1963, long before the days of open adoption, so I knew very little about my start in life. I knew only that I had been born to a young, single woman who, in the terms used at that time, "had given me up for adoption." Given me up.

You know that nasty little voice that you hear in the back of your head? The one that tells you that you're not smart enough, pretty enough, etc. Fill in the blank for the one that really makes you feel the worst about yourself. That is Satan trying to draw you away from God. He told me, "You think you are so special? Well, you're not! As a matter of fact, you are a big fake! You are a mistake. God didn't plan you. You happened because two people did something they shouldn't have done. It was wrong and, as a result, you are wrong." Those words rang in my head over and over and over again, throughout the years.

How do you silence that evil voice? The only way is to turn to God, the Voice of Truth. At the first women's retreat I had ever attended, the speaker had us list the negative words we hear about ourselves. Then she sent us to our rooms with Bibles to find God's words that pertained to us. I didn't really know where to begin, so I went to Psalms, my favorite book. I paged aimlessly until, suddenly, words jumped out of the page at me:

"You made all the delicate, inner parts of my body and knit me together in my mother's womb. Thank you for making me so wonderfully complex! Your workmanship is marvelous— and how well I know it. You watched me as I was being formed in utter seclusion, as I was woven together in the dark of the womb." (Psalm 139:13-15 NLT)

The tears started to pour down my cheeks as a new realization hit me. **I was not a mistake! I was just mistaken.** God *was* there when I was conceived. He planned me even if the couple whose DNA I carry did not.

You are not the momentary whim of a careless creator experimenting in the laboratory of life...You were made with a purpose.

Og Mandino

What words define you? Who is the source of those words? Take those words and check their accuracy against the Voice of Truth in the Bible.

Jesus,

You are the Voice of Truth. Silence that voice that tries to tell me that I am less than who You created me to be. Show me who You created me to be, Your marvelous workmanship!

Amen.

Something to think about...

Draw a vertical line down the center of a piece of paper.

On the left side, list the negative words you believe define you.

On the right side, list the words God chooses to define you.
(Psalms is a great place to start!)

Kelsey's First Day of School
(2001)

Our Words Matter

It was Kelsey's first day of school. First grade. A monumental moment for children—and their parents. Kelsey and her mom had spent hours shopping for the perfect dress. ("What are you going to wear on the first day of school?" It's part of the ritual, right?) They found a darling dress with matching purse and headband.

Kelsey's enthusiasm for starting school was over-the-top. She brought that eagerness with her that first day, along with her shiny notebook and pencil box. She entered the classroom, wearing her new outfit—each of the little scholars anxiously wondered about each other. As she got to her desk, one of the other girls said, critically, "Why are you wearing that? You look like you're going to church."

In a matter of moments, Kelsey's excitement turned to embarrassment and self-consciousness. The put-down by another 7-year-old girl had dampened her spirit and changed her view of this new experience. The words hurt.

Children say hurtful things, and it's easy to chalk it up to immaturity. Adults say hurtful things, and it's easy to chalk it up to…what? We sure can't blame it on immaturity. We're old enough to know better. And yet, we hear disrespectful and hurtful conversations in our workplaces, our homes, and even our churches every day.

The author of the book of James wasn't kidding when he wrote, *"Likewise, the tongue is a small part of the body, but it makes great boasts. Consider what a great forest is set on fire by a small spark. The tongue also is a fire, a world of evil among the parts of the body. It corrupts the whole person, sets the whole course of his life on fire, and is itself set on fire by hell...with the tongue we praise our Lord and Father, and with it we curse men, who have been made in God's likeness. Out of the same mouth comes praise and cursing. My brothers, this should not be."* (James 3:5-6, 9-10)

Sometimes our hurtful words show up in statements of anger. Other times they show up in gossip, behind-the-back conversations, or simply the sarcastic put-down. At other times, the words we intend to be funny or witty cross the line, and nobody leaves the conversation feeling good about what was said. Most of the time, "being mean" is not the intent. However, like children, the words that sting our hearts just feel...mean.

A great woman of faith, missionary, and author, Amy Carmichael, said, "If, in any way, I belittle those who I am called to serve...if I can easily discuss the shortcomings or the sins of any man or woman...then I know nothing of Calvary's love." Her statement challenges me every time I read it.

> *If, in any way, I belittle those who I am called to serve... if I can easily discuss the shortcomings or the sins of any man or woman...then I know nothing of Calvary's love.*
>
> *Amy Carmichael*

Oh, it is so easy to get caught up in conversations about other people's business, isn't it? Likewise, to be swept away by the drama and emotion created when someone has stumbled. We start to hear bits and pieces of someone's tragedy or failings, and it's like a bad accident. We're transfixed; we can't turn away. Too often we quickly become experts on what really happened, or why something bad has happened, and our words keep fueling a fire that should be extinguished rather than fanned.

It's during those moments that we need to go back to our Sunday School or Vacation Bible School days and remember what we were taught in the song, "O Be Careful Little Eyes."

"O be careful little eyes what you see.
O be careful little ears what you hear.
O be careful little hands what you do.
O be careful little feet where you go.
O be careful little mouth what you say."

The lesson? Be careful! We have control over our participation in *any* type of conversation. Our tone, words, actions, and decisions should be mindful and intentional. Why? The song continues, "There's a Father up above, and He's looking down in love." God hears our every word. *And* he is listening with the loving ears of a Father who wants us to choose to do the right thing.

Remember, our words matter. Let's choose them wisely.

"Sticks and stones may break my bones, but words will never hurt me." (What a silly rhyme.)

Oh, gracious Lord,

   Please forgive me for the times that my words have been hurtful. Forgive me for even trying to excuse them—"I was tired. Sad. Stressed." My words are still my words. Please continue to work on my heart, since that is the wellspring of my words. God, please show me how I can use my words every day to encourage someone, help someone, or bring someone comfort. "May the words of my mouth and the meditation of my heart be pleasing in your sight, O Lord my Rock, and my Redeemer." (Psalm 19:14)

                                    Amen.

Doodle Page...

Who would be blessed by your kind words today?

God hears your
cry and has
the power and
compassion to
rescue you.

Swimming Against the Waves

I wouldn't call myself a great swimmer. Childhood swimming lessons at the pool in Crookston, Minn. and at Lake Linka in Starbuck, Minn., prepared me to stroke, crawl, and float—as long as the water is calm. It's when the water gets rough and wavy that I experience trouble.

When I was about 10 years old, I went to Camp Fire Girls' Camp. I had never been in a canoe. However, to use one, I had to take a swimming test that required my going out on the lake alone, flipping the canoe, and saving myself. Good grief. This was just a bad "idea" from the start.

Things started out fine, but then, the storm clouds came rolling in. Just as I was prepared to flip my canoe, the wind picked up, and the rain began. I looked at the lifeguard on the beach, monitoring my test from the shoreline. Clearly, she wasn't going to show me any mercy and call it quits because of the weather. This was a real "Save yourself or die!" moment. (OK. That's a bit dramatic, but, you get what I mean, right?)

My panic wasn't drama, it was *real*. I flailed my arms and jerked my legs trying to keep my head above the waves. Certainly, I gulped half the lake into my tightening stomach. Fish fled, and turtles buried themselves in the mud to avoid my frantic antics. Throughout this terror, I prayed that God would miraculously stop the wind and rain and gently place me on top of the up-ended canoe. I vaguely remember wishing that I had forsaken all vanity and worn the nose plugs. No way was I prepared to take on those stormy waters.

As I think back to that terrifying event, I wonder what kind of person could have faced those waves with more confidence (and elegance) than I displayed. Maybe Dara Torres. I bet she wouldn't have let that storm get the best of her. After all, Dara is the fastest female swimmer in America today. She has competed in five Olympic Games, winning 12 medals. Dana has the strength to do more than dog paddle and pant when the waves are high. In fact she probably could have lifted the canoe with one arm above her head while swimming to shore in the pelting rain and gusty winds. Why? She has studied. Practiced. Trained.

And yet…
There are some waves that not even Dara Torres can handle. The best of the best can't swim forever in waves that capsize ships the length of several football fields. (My waves weren't quite that high, but they might as well have been.) The same principle applies to life's stormy waters.

There are some waves we can't conquer, no matter how trained or disciplined we are. We can't practice caring for a parent with dementia. There's no training for the emotional devastation of losing our home. And, all the discipline in the world won't guarantee cancer-free bodies.

What then?

"In my distress I called to the Lord; I cried to my God for help… He reached down from on high and took hold of me; he drew me out of deep waters." (Psalm 18:6, 16)

Picture this.

We're struggling to catch our breath in the middle of the lake, waves crashing in on every side of us. We're keeping our heads above the water, just barely. The current continues to pull us in a downward spiral. Now, all that remains are our faces, staring up in panic at the dark, disinterested skies; we no longer have the strength to hold our heads upright. Then, our bodies begin to sink into the murky depths... YES! At that very moment the heavens part, and God's strong arm reaches down and scoops us out of the deep water. (Don't you just love this scene? At least the end of it?)

This imagery hardly matches the real intensity in which God rescues us. The Psalm isn't presenting us with a gentle fisherman who just happens to be boating by at the right time with a fish net. No! It says "The earth trembled and quaked...He parted the heavens and came down...He mounted the cherubim and flew...Clouds advanced, with hailstones and bolts of lightning...The Lord thundered from heaven; the voice of the Most High resounded." This is a God who was on a mission. He would rescue us.

God is ALWAYS bigger than our situation. HE will get us through ANY storm.

What waves are crashing around you today? Death? Disease? A runaway child? Loss of a job? Heartbreak and anguish so intense that you feel it as physical pain in your chest? Nothing is too big for Him. *Not any thing!*

Remember, God hears your cry, and He has the power and compassion to rescue you. Stop fighting the strong currents that buffet you. Let God reach down and draw you to Himself. Say, "Yes, God."

Well, somehow I made it to shore, no thanks to the "lifeguard" who was oblivious to my need. I didn't go back out in a canoe during that whole week at camp. No thank you.

God didn't promise us an easy life. He promised only that He would always be with us. God promised to rescue us, and, in my lifetime, God has never failed me.

> *The problem many of us have is that our God is too small. We are not convinced that we are absolutely safe in the hands of a fully competent, all-knowing, ever-present God.*
>
> *John Ortberg*

Oh, God,

   Please reach down and pull me out of the waves.   Help me to trust you.   Give me the courage to stop struggling, and let my heart and my weary body rest in your arms. Please slow my beating heart and give me your peace.

   Thank you.

                                        Amen.

*Friends and Family with Scottie Benedict
Homecoming 2011*

How many of us lead a life on the
sidelines of the greatest life God
yearns to give us because we have
taken our own path? We settle for
crumbs and miss out on the feast.

Kathy Troccoli

God and My Game of Life

I love football. As a little girl, one of my most cherished times of the week was watching the Sunday afternoon games with my dad. It was part of a routine. After church, our family would have dinner on the nice china at the living room table, and discuss how the choir sounded that morning. Then, we'd all take a Sunday afternoon nap. (Julie, Lori, and I would sleep in our slips. I don't know why—they were very uncomfortable as sleepwear.) I wouldn't sleep too long. I'd quietly crawl out of bed while my sisters still slept, knowing dad would be sitting in his big chair downstairs in the den, watching the Minnesota Vikings try and beat their opponent. I'd take the chair next to his. We'd each have a bowl of vanilla ice cream covered with Hershey's chocolate syrup, and we'd cheer for our beloved team. I can still feel the absolute joy and complete contentment that came from spending that time with him.

My heart still bleeds purple for my Vikings. But, my favorite quarterback? Scottie Benedict. No contest. He has never played for the Vikings, but he is my favorite athlete to watch on the field, and he is my favorite youngest nephew. I watched his Minnetonka Skipper high school games live online. However, for the homecoming game his senior year, we all cleared our calendars and showed up. It was one of the best football games I've ever experienced.

Our family, extended family, and friends cheered, yelled at the refs, high-fived, and laughed while we watched him lead his team to victory. We couldn't have been more excited (or louder) when his passes were completed and the touchdowns were made. When he got sacked, we stopped breathing. When he wasn't on the field, we watched him on the sidelines. Nothing was more important than Scottie that evening. We were completely focused on him. No other player mattered (unless it was a big defensive end running straight for him).

I bet that's how God watches us. He is completely focused on our every decision, action, touchdown, and fumble. **He cares for us, celebrates with us, and hurts with us.** What a great image. Not only is God in the stands calling our names and cheering for us...

He's calling our plays.

He's running with us down the field.

He's picking us up when we get hit hard.

He's blocking for us when the big guys are driving.

He's getting us back in the game when we drop the ball.

He's giving us high-fives.

You see, God wants us to play every game—live every day—FULL OUT. *"Now what I am commanding you today is not too difficult for you or beyond your reach...See, I set before you today life and prosperity, death and destruction. For I command you today to love the Lord your God, to walk in his ways, and to keep his commands, decrees and laws; then you will live and increase, and the Lord your God will bless you in the land you are entering to possess...Now choose life..."* (Deuteronomy 30: 11, 15-16, 19)

"I have come that they may have life, and have it to the full." (John 10:10)

Remember, God tells us to choose life. And, like the game of football, every play—every day—is filled with something new. Sometimes, we carry the ball; other times our friends need some blocking. Plays are called that we disagree with. There are rules to follow. Fans can get unruly. Refs make bad calls. Our team wins some, and we lose some. How cool that God is with us every play of the game.

Have you asked God to play in this game of life with you? He wants to. As your coach, He makes the rules very simple—walk in his ways, and keep his commands. However, he doesn't holler the plays to you from the sideline. He's on the field with you. He knows exactly what you need to make it through the game with a win. Get in the game.

God,
Thank you for caring about every single minute of my game..my life. Thank you for knowing the game plan. Thank you for making it clear to me. Please protect me from the hits that come my way, and give me strength when my energy is spent. And now, dear God, about those Vikings...

Teri Johnson

Teri's Book
"Overcoming The Nevers"

Dry Wells

By Teri Johnson

What is a dry well? Simply put, it's a well that no longer produces, one that has no water. No one returns to a dry well to quench their thirst. In most cases, a dry well would be capped off, abandoned, and forgotten. But, it would not disappear.

Getting water from a well is not an easy task. It takes a massive amount of work. I'm not talking about the modern day technology kind of well that's used by cities, allowing residents to get hot or cold water from our faucets; not that kind of well. I'm talking about the old wells, you know, the ones with a rope and the bucket hanging there. You have to manually turn a crank, lowering the bucket down to the water, scooping the water into the bucket, and then, cranking the bucket to raise it to the surface. That's a lot of work for just one bucket of water!

If you were to make the effort to go to the well, the old fashioned kind, put the bucket on the hook, crank it all the way down to the bottom and then, crank it back up only to find it empty, would your need be met? Would you be able to quench your thirst or use the water to wash your clothes? Bathe yourself or your child? No.

You would most likely walk away feeling sad, defeated, frustrated, dirty, and definitely thirsty. Knowing the well was dry, would you go back to get more water? Perhaps. After all, maybe the well just happened to be dry on that particular day. Maybe tomorrow it will be different. Maybe, because it rained, there will be water in the well.

So, the next day you go to the same well, drop down the same bucket, only to find that the well is still dry. Shoot! Once again your needs are not met. You walk away with the same feelings you had the day before; sad, defeated, frustrated, dirty, and even more thirsty.

This could go on for days with you hoping to get different results. Until, one day, you finally make the decision to accept the reality that the well is dry. It will no longer meet your needs. So, you let it go. You look for another well to meet your needs. The change in your behavior and thinking is very difficult and takes a lot of time.

Over the past couple of years, I've asked myself why in the world I am continually drawn to "dry wells." Now, I'm talking about people and relationships.

> *Expecting others to change just because I want them to change is unrealistic and wishful thinking. We can't make others change, we can only change ourselves.*
>
> Teri Johnson

I make the connection between the two because some of the relationships I've had, or currently have, are like dry wells. They *do not quench my thirst*. I continue going to the person or the "relationship," thinking the next time will be different; but it's not. I leave sad, defeated, sometimes insecure, feeling judged, frustrated, empty, and thirsting for something more.

I've come to the realization, once again, that we, indeed, are creatures of habit. Change is not easy! What have I done? I've taken the path of least resistance, in some cases, and have continued to get the same results. I've kept circling the same mountain, expecting to get different results. Each time, I experience more pain, more hurt.

The truth is, sometimes we have to set aside, or walk away from, the unhealthy to allow God to bring us the healthy. Why is this concept so difficult to grasp and implement? Because we want so desperately for the "well," a.k.a. person or relationship, to not be dry. And, because it's easy to avoid de-cluttering our lives, and to resign ourselves to live "status quo"—even though "status quo" is unhealthy and painful. Additionally, if we choose to let go of something, even though it's unhealthy, what do we replace it with in the meantime?

The question is, do we trust God to bring us healthy? Do we trust that His plans for us are for good, to prosper us, and not to harm us, but to give us hope and a future? (Jeremiah 29:11) If we are clinging to the unhealthy, we will miss opportunities to be blessed with health.

Remember, people and relationships, like a dried up well, remain. As we make the decision to "set aside the unhealthy to make room for the healthy" it doesn't mean we need to destroy or eliminate. We simply don't need to resort to the unhealthy anymore. We need to set boundaries and make room for God to bring us health.

So, how many dry wells are you clinging to?

Dear Father,

Thank you for caring about my relationships. Thank you for wanting me to enjoy relationships that bring me joy, peace, and health. Please help me discern when a relationship is heading in the wrong direction, and then give me the strength to set the right boundaries. Thank you for being a well that is never dry, that always quenches my thirst.

Amen.

Doodle Page...

What relationships have become dry wells in your life?
What do you need from your girlfriends
at this time in your life?
Ask them to quench your thirst.

We loved growing up here.

I Will Give You Rest

My mom, sisters, and I entered a new chapter in our lives when my dad died on July 28, 2003. The story line that was subsequently written was not the one we wanted to write. However, it was our story. This new chapter was shaped by deep sadness and extreme weariness as we moved through the grief over dad's death, and mom's heart attack and her strokes a year later. This challenging chapter ended when mom sold our family home in Climax, Minn., to move to an apartment in St. Paul.

Our story began when mom and dad bought the two-story house in 1955 for $1. (Yes, you read that correctly. They bought it for $1.) Talk about a dream mortgage. They moved it from a farm to the edge of town, and that's where we grew up.

As we grew, so did the house. A basement was added, a garage, an entryway, a den, a laundry room, and another bedroom. Why is this relevant? Because not only did it create more space to live in, it created more space for...stuff.

You know, those things of which memories are made. And, stuff needs to be moved when you sell a house. (If you have ever helped someone move out of a home they've lived in for many, many years, you know exactly what I'm talking about!)

My sisters and I faced the challenge of moving mom out of the house, attacking the various duties with great vigor and enthusiasm. We were going to get this project done fast. The moving van was ordered. The storage unit in St. Paul was rented. Shredders were standing by. A dumpster was sitting on the slab, waiting to be filled. We had been saving boxes for weeks. My friend Kim Wegge had delivered chili and chocolate brownies. (Oh, what a friend.) Our husbands were scheduled to be there in four days to help with hauling mom's downsized belongings to St. Paul. Moving mom would be a snap!

Needless to say, our energy and enthusiasm lasted… oh, about seven hours. What started as a vision of spending quality time together as we laughed and reminisced over accumulated memories soon morphed into an extraordinary sense of OVERWHELM. Also, we hadn't prepared ourselves for the emotional journey these preparations required mom to make.

Mom had been a grade school teacher. It seemed to us as if she'd held onto everything—scores of boxes of 30+ years of school papers and homework assignments copied on mimeograph machines. Shelves of books, books, and more books. File cabinets filled with instruction booklets for obsolete black and white TVs, household appliances, and kitchen gadgets. Banker boxes filled with family pictures. Drawers of cassette and video tapes. Christmas cards and letters going back to the 1950's. THERE WAS JUST SO MUCH …STUFF, and mom did not want *anything* thrown out.

We understood that, since mom had lost control of the part of her life that mattered most—meaning, our father—she needed to find something she could still control... disposal of her stuff. That meant she needed to review and discuss each tiny piece of paper, crumpled receipt, faded instruction booklet, and moldy third-grade art assignment. We understood this in our heads. However, our bodies were screaming, "ENOUGH, ALREADY!" Our emotions and physical strength had reached the breaking point. Too much lifting. Too much sorting. Not enough sleep.

Something had to give.

Thus, it all came to a head on a Friday afternoon. Julie, Lori, and I were sitting in the corner of the basement, going through (you guessed it)....stuff. Frustration was high, and spirits were low. Julie had had enough. She yelled out what we all three were thinking, "I hate this stuff!" just as our friend Harlow Grove walked into the room. (What a greeting, right?)

Harlow was one of dad's former high school students. He started renting our farmland after dad retired, and we considered him one of our family's most special friends. He'd come by to see how things were going. (We got him up to speed in record time.)

I complained about the mold. Lori complained about having to sit on a floor where mice had once scampered. (It is a basement in farm country, you know.) Julie just rolled her eyes and tried to explain that we hadn't seen sunlight for 17 hours. Harlow calmly stood in the doorway and patiently waited for us to finish our tirade.

I don't know if it was because we were embarrassed by our outburst, or if we were just so grateful for Harlow's act of kindness—probably both—but we sisters started to laugh. And, we kept laughing. And then, we couldn't stop laughing. We sat on that cold, damp basement floor and just let it all out until the concrete walls reverberated with our hilarious cacophony. The range of emotions we'd been feeling dissolved into laughter and tears. This laughter came from deep within our souls, big tears and heavy sobbing carrying it forward. Then, our exhausted muscles seemed to loosen up. Headaches went away. We weren't so tired anymore. Our burden was lifted.

When Harlow left our little corner of the basement, he went up the stairs, through the kitchen, and into the garage. He saw my husband Steve and said, "Now I know why you're out here."

You've had similar experiences, I'm sure. The loss, heartache, grieving, and physical work that is required to adapt to family changes and the beginning of new chapters are so overwhelming. It makes you weary, doesn't it?

During these times remember…God gives us rest.

"Come to me, all you who are weary and burdened, and I will give you rest. Take my yoke upon you and learn from me, for I am gentle and humble in heart, and you will find rest for your souls. For my yoke is easy and my burden is light." The verses in Matthew 11:28-30 are not just words on a page. They are promises from an Almighty, All-knowing Savior.

HE – the King of Kings, Lord of Lords, and Great Lover of our Souls – HE reaches down and takes us in his strong arms. He holds us in his embrace and says, "Rest here. Let me ease your burden." Oh, what a gift.

Remember, sometimes, Jesus gives us rest through sleep. And, sometimes, He gives us rest through the kind actions of people like Harlow Grove. Harlow stopped by to let us know he cared. He spent time with us. He laughed with us. And then he carried some stuff upstairs for us. Harlow was a God-send.

Trust Jesus. Trust him with your cares. Trust him with your burdens. Trust him with your heart.

His strength is perfect when our strength is gone; He'll carry us when we can't carry on. Raised in His power, the weak become strong; His strength is perfect, His strength is perfect.

Steven Curtis Chapman

What "boxes of stuff" are weighing you down?
Write a prayer, asking God to carry those boxes for you.

Oh, dear Jesus,

My heart is heavy today. I've run out of energy. The decisions are too great. I just can't take another step. Would you please hold me? Please give me physical rest. Rest in my soul. Rest in my heart. Thank you, Jesus, for caring so much about me. Thank you for making my burden lighter.

Thank you.

Amen.

God, Help My Unbelief

God,
I don't understand random acts of violence.
I don't understand people shooting other people because
they disagree with them.
I don't understand children bullying other children.
I don't understand cancer.

These things make me angry, sad,
and I get angry at myself for being angry!

I know you are Trustworthy.
And, I know I should trust you.
Today it is harder to do that
because it is so difficult to believe You are in control.
It is hard to understand why You allow the pain and the
tragedy.

Jesus, please forgive me for my lack of trust.
Please forgive me for my unbelief.
Please give me a heart that remains calm,
knowing that YOU are bigger than anything that happens to
us.

Today I want to hold fast to the promise you made to Joshua
and all of us who have come after him.
"I will never leave you nor forsake you." (Joshua 1:5)
That seems to be the only thing that makes sense…
The only constant.

Jesus, I am depending on your promise.
Amen.

Pam and Barry Boettcher

Our favorite traveling companions.

I'm Lost...Now What

The city map on my lap should have provided clear directions. The street signs in front of us should have coordinated with the map. They didn't. We had to admit that we were lost.

My husband Steve and I were traveling through Sioux City, Iowa, and we really had no clue where we were. And because we didn't know where we were, we weren't sure how to get back on track. Our frustration and anxiety were mounting.

I was navigating and trying to follow the map. Steve was driving and trying to follow my instructions. Our patient traveling companions, Pam and Barry, realized that it was best for them to sit silently in the backseat and pray for a miracle. Steve and I had piloted the car past the same historical site—Floyd Monument—at least three times in the last 25 minutes. It was obvious to all that we were going in circles. Exits were few, and we didn't know which way to turn once we got to the end of the off-ramp. And, on top of all of that confusion, we were stomach-growling hungry.

So Steve and I were in a quandary. Do we trust the map? Street signs? Our common sense? Each other? After a short, pointed, give-and-take (OK. We had some words.), we painstakingly wound our way through the unfamiliar city streets until we eventually reached a familiar landmark.

Sometimes, life is like a confusing drive through strange streets. You're in need of directions. Your journey has unexpectedly taken you down unfamiliar roads, and you want to get your bearings. Whom do you listen to? What do you depend on? Which road map do you follow? The bottom-line answer: God's heart. God's heart will never, ever lead you down the wrong road. This promise is one of the greatest gifts He offers.

So, where do you find His heart? You find it in His Word, through prayer, and in talking with Him. Why can you depend on God's heart? He's already proven to you why. Look at the cross. That's how much He loves you.

Christian songwriter and singer, Stormie Omartian, is one of my favorite authors. In her book, *Just Enough LIGHT for the Step I'm On*, she writes,

"It doesn't matter what your situation is at this moment. Wherever you are, God has a path for you that is filled with good things. Draw close to Him, and you'll find it. Say, '*Show me the way in which I should walk and the thing I should do*' (Jeremiah 42:3). He will do that and, if you carefully follow as He guides you, He will not let you get off the path. With each step He will reveal more of Himself. '*Your ears shall hear a word*

> *As you take one step at a time, holding God's hand and letting Him lead, He will get you where you need to go.*
>
> Stormie Omartian

behind you, saying, 'This is the way, walk in it' (Isaiah 30:21). So reach up right now and take God's hand. He promises He won't let you fall."

God's heart will never, ever lead you down the wrong road.

Doesn't His constancy just make the journey feel a little easier? Remember, we have a God who *wants* to show us where to go. He *wants* to lead us to good things. He *wants* us to take his hand and walk with him. This truth is just so amazing.

It was terribly frustrating, to get lost in Sioux City, Iowa. We had maps and street signs on that trip, and still, we strayed from the correct path. Losing our way in life—without any physical road map to set in front of us—can be terrifying. Thanks be to God who is our mapmaker, travel agent, and constant companion. He shows us where to go, one step at a time….all the while walking by our sides.

Psalm 25:4-5 says, *"Show me your ways, O Lord, teach me your paths; guide me in your truth and teach me, for you are God my Savior, and my hope is in you all day long."*

God's heart.
It's the best guide ever.

Dear God,

Today I am grateful that you always know where I should be going, and you always know how to get me there. Thank you for being my road map, street sign, and travel guide. Please help me to listen carefully for your directions.

Amen.

Something to think about...

Mark an X on the lower left corner of the Doodle Page and label it Point A (your current reality).

Mark an X in the upper right corner of the Doodle Page and label it Point B (your ideal life).

Between Point A and Point B, note the areas of your life where you'd like guidance (e.g., finances, job, career, etc.) .

Ask God for the roadmap that will get you from Point A to Point B.

Doodle Page...

Shabbot

Shabbat

By Donna Fagerstrom

"... Jesus often withdrew to lonely places..." (Luke 5:16)

My husband and I were raised in a quaint little town on the shores of Lake Michigan. Today some of our best memories include swimming, boating, water-skiing, and more. Soon after we were married we agreed that owning a boat would be a sacrifice we were willing to make. I'm sure you're saying, "sacrifice?" Well, in our early years of marriage, it really was a sacrifice, and it was also, so worth the investment. We found rest and refreshment not only for us but for all the people we delighted in sharing that recreational time with us. Sometimes, the boat was our "lonely place" away from the pace.

Those early years brought many opportunities to teach energetic teenagers in our church youth group how to water-ski. Then, came the years of spinning around the lake with screaming kids on inner-tubes, followed by the barefoot water-skiers, knee-boarders, and on goes the list. It was a renewing time. Throughout our married life, this is where we were restored on our weekly day off and warm summer nights, with the exception being when we lived in Colorado. The one reservoir available to us just didn't cut it.

When we purchased the first boat large enough to sleep on (tight and cozy, more than not), our daughter Darci would have a friend spend the night or a vacation week with us. In our cramped quarters, I loved hearing the giggles and chatter as the girls talked into the night until sleep overtook them. As Darci grew into her high school and college years, "going out to the boat" became a great way to entertain her friends. The best part was that we had a *captured* audience; nobody could go anywhere…we were together! Together, we played and laughed. Together, we talked and prayed. Together, we shared the best of meaningful memories.

Sabbath-rest has always been an important priority for me. Getting away from the busyness and routines of life are vitally important to my body, soul, and mind. I need to spend alone time with God, "time apart" to renew and restore what is weary and worn.

> *If we fail to stop and draw from His fresh, infinite supply of mercy and grace, we will find ourselves having to operate out of our own depleted, meager resources.*
>
> *Nancy DeMoss*

It's customary that a boat has a name. We went without naming our floating retreat for a few years and were often asked, "What's your boat's name?" We decided on "3-D," which captured our first names' initials for **D**oug, **D**onna and **D**arci. It was a fitting name, and one we enjoyed. However, when our daughter became engaged, she asked the inevitable question—"What about Jay and the name of our boat?" My husband teased, "We're not changing the name." She responded back, "Dad, Jay doesn't start with a "D." A new name was born, and it was Jay, our soon-to-become son-in-love, who actually helped us to collaborate and arrive at the name "Shabbot."

"Shabbot?" It is a simple play on words taking Sabbath (Hebrew, "Shabbat") and combining it with the word Boat that creatively gives us **Shabbot**. It is our place of personal Sabbath—a place apart, a place for just us and God. While many friends have enjoyed Shabbot with us, it will never replace our time of worship with the body of Jesus. It is simply our little place of rest, renewal, and revival for our very lives.

Jesus often had to make time for rest (Matthew 14:23; Mark 1:35; John 6:15). He removed himself to quiet mountain places. Several times he declared that he was going to get away for a time to be with his Father. It was important to slow down the pace and get away from the demands upon Him—to rest, to pray, to refresh. Sometimes, he said to the disciples, let's get in the boat and go to the other side. Those became holy (set apart) times.

We have made a place of rest on Shabbot. Where is your place to renew and restore your walk with God and others? It does not need to be a boat or cottage. One

> *Jesus said to them, 'Come with me by yourselves to a quiet place and get some rest.'*
>
> *Mark 6:31*

friend finds solace and peace by walking out to a favorite lighthouse and reviving her soul in that place. Another friend has a quiet, peaceful corner, surrounded by plants and trees, in which to commune with her Creator. One couple finds their place-apart by driving every year along the hundreds of miles of the Great Lakes shoreline. Others go for reviving walks. Some visit unfamiliar places.

I don't know what your personal Sabbath looks like. I humbly encourage you to "make one" if you don't already have one. Seek the Lord for an answer as to a place and time you will "set apart" for rest and renewal. We can't live well without it.

Father,

Thank you that you have modeled Sabbath rest for us. Thank you for the lonely places, places set apart, that you provide. Help me to be faithful in disciplining myself to rest and refresh. Without this time, I can't serve you well or minister to others. Thank you for the gift of "Shabbot, and the rest, refreshment, and renewal it provides for my family and others. Your love and creation never cease to amaze me. Thank you for providing the opportunity to enjoy both each and every day.

Amen.

Vicki's Girls
Gaye, Julie, Anita
Lori, Alana

Vicki's Girls

My sisters and I sang together in a number of churches when we were younger. Dad was often invited to be a guest speaker, and we would provide the "special music." Julie and Lori had better voices than I did, but I could accompany our trio on the piano and find the harmony. We sounded pretty good. Or, at least I thought we did. One afternoon as we practiced—all three of us squirming to fit on the piano bench—Julie nudged her elbow into my side and said, "Come on, Gaye. Sing nice." I thought I had been.

When the Lucky Leaf 4-H Club organized in Climax, we teamed up with two sisters and good friends, Anita and Alana Grove, and formed the musical group, Vicki's Girls. (Vicki Irwin was the head of our 4-H Club; she thought the name was exquisite. I had hoped we'd be called The 5 Blonde Bombshells.) We competed in 4-H competitions and performed at conventions and events, singing pop songs and show tunes like "Chattanooga Shoe Shine Boy," "Boogie Woogie Bugle Boy," and "Sisters."

Vicki's Girls was invited one summer to perform for an event at Moorhead State University. As we were getting dressed backstage, our excitement about the program turned into complete horror. Julie and I had forgotten our bras. (We were wearing summer tanks with built-in bras, which is why we didn't notice it earlier. This is probably more information than you wanted to know, but it helps explain our dilemma.)

Although there was not a lot of undergarment support needed—if you know what I mean—the idea of going bra-less was just unthinkable. And to make matters even more disastrous, we had forgotten our matching white sandals.

So what did we do? We sent dad on a mission. The command was given—bring back bras and white sandals! Dad didn't think twice about it. He jumped in the Ford LTD and hit the road for the West Acres shopping mall.

Unfortunately, we had forgotten to tell him what size bras and shoes we needed.

Dad came back with six bras—nothing smaller than a DD cup. And the sandals? Sizes 9 and 10. Bless his heart. He had really tried. Julie and I chose the bras that seemed to work the best, and we wore our everyday brown sandals on stage.

What I remember most about that day is dad's firm commitment to solving our problem. I mean, really. There aren't many fathers who cheerfully go on a hot summer's day into the lingerie department at Sears to buy bras! He cared so much about us—our needs, our happiness, and our teenage vulnerability. His love knew no limitations.

Love is demonstrated in many ways. We feel it in our daily interactions. We experience it through written messages and conversations. In words, actions, smiles, and yes, even in the "bra shopping," we are reminded that we are loved.

I was very fortunate to grow up with parents who loved me unconditionally and sisters who loved me most of the time. (We were sisters, you know.) And yet, their love doesn't begin to measure up to the breadth and depth of God's love for me. Nothing demonstrates it more definitively than our Savior's death on the cross. *"For God so loved the world that he gave his one and only Son, that whoever believes in him shall not perish but have eternal life."* (John 3:16)

Remember, not only does God know our shapes, our shoe size, and our insecurities, He knows how many hairs we have on our head. He knows our dreams, our desires, our hurts, and our joys. He knows our hearts.

What a gift—an all-knowing Heavenly Father who understands us and cares about us during our time on earth, and a Savior who graces us with eternal life when our days on earth end. How can our "thank you's" ever be enough?

I am reminded of one of my favorite songs, "My Tribute," words and music by André Crouch. I leave the words with you as my closing prayer.

Dear Lord,

"How can I say thanks for the things you have done for me? Things so undeserved, yet You gave to prove your love for me. The voices of a million angels could not express my gratitude. All that I am and ever hope to be, I owe it all to thee. To God be the glory."

Aunt Idelle!

Meet my Aunt Idelle!

Meet my aunt, Idelle (Nornes) Bagne. She is 85 years old, lives in an apartment for senior citizens in Detroit Lakes, Minn., AND she's got more life in her than the Energizer Bunny®.

Nothing keeps Aunt Idelle from getting the most out of every moment she takes a breath. She's still serving, teaching, serving, laughing, serving, and helping. (Did I mention "serving?")

Take a glance at her weekly schedule:
Monday mornings she volunteers at the hospital for the terminally ill. She leads a devotional on Tuesday mornings. As president of the tenant's group for her senior community, she's responsible for the social hour every Wednesday afternoon. Finally, every Monday and Wednesday she leads an exercise class for a group of fabulous women. (Idelle taught health and physical education in the public school system for many years.)

Who attends her exercise class? Not your typical group! You won't find spandex-clad athletes. Instead you'll meet:
Gladys, who has a hernia.
Margaret, whose left leg "doesn't work real well."
Alice, who has frequent dizzy spells.
Catherine, who has painful osteoporosis.
And Nora, who has plastic arteries in her left leg, an

artificial right leg, two kinds of cancer, and is blind.

Aunt Idelle calls them her "miracle class."

The Miracle Class gets together twice a week to work on balance, range of motion, and a little bit of strengthening. During their workouts, they talk about their families and tell jokes. I think they're really working on living—physically, emotionally, mentally, and spiritually.

Many of us have found it way too easy to complain about life's troubles. Every headache, stubbed toe, and sniffle becomes THE DAILY TOPIC OF CONVERSATION for anyone who will listen. (There are days when I could carry the banner and lead the parade on this whining.) I believe the more we complain, the bigger our problems become. Then, at some point, what we're complaining about takes on a life of its own. We have moved so far away from living with joy. Instead, if we'd take a few moments to realize how good we really have it, our attitude would change, and we'd start enjoying life a whole lot more.

Today is the day that the Lord has made. You don't have to grin and bear it. You don't have to drag yourself out of bed and dread the day. There is so much life awaiting you. His Life. Breathe it in. Live like you mean it!

Kathy Troccoli

Getting to a mental and spiritual place where we live from abundance, where we live fully present and joyfully in the moment, doesn't require a lot of money or time. It can begin for you, simply, with an accounting of your blessings. Do you have a roof over your head? Write it down. Can you read this book? Write it down. Do you have one friend? Write it down. If you can't think of any blessings, ask the person next to you—stranger or friend—to tell you three things you can be grateful for. Creating your list is as simple as that, and reflecting upon it will change the direction of your attitude and your life.

Of course, this focus on living intentionally can be taken to the extreme. Some time ago I drove through a carwash. Above the entrance there was a very large sign that read, "Please be Alive...Alert... Awake... & Enthusiastic AT ALL TIMES during your car wash experience." Really? For Heaven's sake, it's a car wash!

> *Rather than asking yourself what you feel like doing, ask yourself: 'What needs to be done?'*
>
> *Steve Chandler*

Aunt Idelle's Miracle Class at the senior citizen's apartment building in Detroit Lakes has found a way of living each moment to its fullest. How are you showing up for life today? Are you living as if each moment counts?

"This is the day the Lord has made; let us rejoice and be glad in it." (Psalm 118:24)

Oh, Jesus,

Thank you for today. Thank you for all the joys and blessings that are just waiting to be discovered. Thank you for making it possible for me to live from a place of joyful abundance. Please remind me how much good is in my life...how much I have to be thankful for. Thank you for creating each day as a gift to us.

Amen.

Doodle Page...

Make a list of 50 blessings in your life. (Yes…50.)
Thank God for each one.

Fabulous piano!

(1975)

From Fear to Faith

It is unfortunate, but true. Too often, fear is a central character in our stories—the paralyzing fear of man, the fear of losing our job, making mistakes, not being good enough.

During my senior year in high school, I presented a full piano recital. I had worked on the program for four years. It required memorizing and playing about 90 minutes of music—from Bach and Beethoven to Gershwin and Debussy. The recital was held in a beautiful church, equipped with a shiny, black Steinway piano.

As my piano teacher introduced me, I stood in a little alcove at the front of the church. I wanted to run; I was so nervous. The fear and anxiety I felt that afternoon are still as potent today as if I'd experienced them yesterday. A back door to a fire escape offered a way out. I remember the exact moment when I decided to move through my fear, sit down, and play that baby grand. I'm so grateful I did.

Worrying about not playing well or forgetting a few piano notes pales in comparison to worrying about health issues, unemployment, or matters of the heart. And yet, there is great comfort knowing that God is with us through all the daily fears and the life-changing fears. *"...Be strong and courageous. Do not be terrified; do not be discouraged, for the Lord your God will be with you wherever you go."* (Joshua 1:9)

I have been learning much from Max Lucado's book, *Fearless: Imagine Your Life without Fear*. As Lucado lists the fears that keep so many of us up at night (e.g., the fear of disappointing God, overwhelming challenges, not mattering, and life's final moments, etc.), he constantly reminds us that Jesus said, "*Do not be afraid.*"

> *Fear will always knock on the door. Just don't invite it in for dinner, and for heaven's sake, don't offer it a bed for the night.*
>
> *Max Lucado*

Remember, when Jesus said, "Do not be afraid," he meant it. He has given me the provisions, the tools, and the resources, to turn from fear to faith. God would never tell me, or you, to do something impossible, right?

A constant state of fear is an ugly place in which to live and work. Nothing good comes of it. Being afraid of the unknown does not give us more control of our situation, it just makes us feel rotten. And, it steals our joy. Lucado writes, "Fear itself is not a sin. But it can lead to sin…Fear may fill our world, but it doesn't have to fill our hearts. It will always knock on the door. Just don't invite it in for dinner, and for heaven's sake, don't offer it a bed for the night."

Christian singer and author, Stormie Omartian, writes, "Any sign of fear should always be a call to prayer. The moment you feel it, draw immediately close to God. Get a sense of his presence and leading and allow His love to fully penetrate the situation."

God's Word. God's voice. God's presence. They are powerful enough to remove all fear and gentle enough to soothe our souls. I like that.

What will you do today to move from fear to faith? Ask God to meet you at your place of anxiety, worry, and fear. Ask Him to replace those thoughts with his promises, his peace. He wants to do that, you know.

> *Any sign of fear should always be a call to prayer. The moment you feel it, draw immediately close to God.*
>
> Stormie Omartian

Dear God,

Thank you for being so much bigger than anything I'm worried about. Thank you for caring about my daily worries and decisions, and for those things in life that draw the breath right out of me. Please show me where I need to replace fear with faith. Please give me the strength to meditate on the things that bring me peace and hope. Thank you for taking care of me.

Amen.

Doodle Page...

Draw a vertical line down the center of this page.
On the left, list those fears that keep you awake at night.
On the right, list God's promises to remove those fears—
whatever you need at this moment.

Hello from Climax, Minnesota

Our Unfounded Fears

There aren't a lot of things that get the people in my hometown of Climax, Minn., riled up. We are, for the most part, stoic Scandinavian farmers who care about family, the land, church, education, and the weather. But, back in the spring of 1970, our peaceful little community was threatened by college students, and people were uneasy.

Here's what was behind our anxiety. We'd heard about the destruction inflicted on Zap, North Dakota, (population 250) the year before, when 3,000 college students descended on this small town for a "Zip to Zap" weekend. (Who hadn't heard about it? The story led the *CBS Evening News with Walter Cronkite*, and it went down as the only official riot in the state of North Dakota that had to be quelled by the National Guard.) What started as an alternative destination for North Dakota State University students who didn't want to go to Ft. Lauderdale during spring break, ultimately became a national attraction for thousands of students looking for a good time. Large quantities of alcohol were consumed, resulting in some big behavioral issues. (I'm putting that nicely.) When the two small taverns in town ran out of alcohol, well, you can probably guess how upset the students got. And, I don't think I need to tell you what happens when there aren't enough bathrooms to accommodate 3,000 students' natural bodily functions and the results of excessive drinking. Someone started a bonfire in the middle of Main Street, and the townspeople feared for their safety. The

National Guard was called in. It was all just plain ugly.

So, when our community leaders heard that last year's Zip to Zap was going to be this year's Clip to Climax, (or Come to Climax, as some of my friends remember it), they took the threat very seriously. Precautionary plans were made to safeguard property, protect the children, and keep things as peaceful as possible. Businesses bordered up their windows, and the men in town signed up in shifts for patrolling. It was a big deal.

But, first things first. Since the Zap event was the town's only frame of reference, and nobody really knew what to expect, most families decided that their children would stay with friends in the country over that weekend. Julie, Lori, and I were going to stay at my classmate's Coleen's house—that would be fun. We were excited about riding the school bus with her after school on Friday.

Things were pretty calm in our household leading up to the weekend, until Thursday night. Julie, Lori, and I were in Lori's bedroom, looking out the window for any indications that hoodlums had started to arrive. We could see clear down main street from Lori's window—the full length of the town. As we peered into the dark night, our thrill-seeking curiosity turned to fear. We saw smoke coming out of the windows of the Corner Café at the other end of town. Julie whispered slowly and deliberately, "This is just the beginning. They're going to burn every building in town until they get to our house and then, they're going to set ours on fire." Well, 5-year-old Lori burst into tears, I started yelling at Julie for saying such a scary thing, and we all three tumbled over each other on our way down the stairs, screaming at the top of our lungs. We were convinced death was five blocks away and moving in on us fast.

Our fear was unfounded. A few quick phone calls revealed there was a small grease fire on the café's grill, resulting in billows of smoke. It had been quickly put out with a small fire extinguisher.

Other fears were also unfounded. It rained all weekend, and the cold, miserable conditions weren't very welcoming. The expected "Hell's Angels" agitators looked more like hippies—all 25 of them. That's right. No more than 25 rowdies showed up. One of the uninvited guests used the street as his biffy. Perhaps that's because a few of his friends had burned the outhouse in our park. Those are the only stories we have to tell from the non-event. There had been nothing to fear.

Our fears. So many of them are unfounded. It is easy to take a spark of concern and create a firestorm of doubt, dread, panic, and terror. So much of our anxiety can be prevented if we would simply stop processing the potential scenarios. Our child fails a test in school; she will never find a job. We have the sniffles; pneumonia will take our lives in a matter of weeks. Our husband is late coming home from work; his car stalled and he's been kidnapped by not-so-Good Sammaritans. We create our own worst case scenarios.

So do not fear, for I am with you; do not be dismayed, for I am your God.

Isaiah 41:10

"Be still, and know that I am God." (Psalms 46:10) This Biblical passage is key to keeping our fears in perspective and maintaining a peaceful heart. Instead of letting our thoughts create a dramatic story that will probably never become reality, let's stop for a moment. Let's ask God to check our thoughts, and ask for protection for our hearts and our emotions. Let's ask Him to help us keep our situation in perspective, and then, walk through it with us as it unfolds in real time. Doesn't that seem like a much calmer approach?

What fears do you keep hidden in your heart? What scares you? Why is it so difficult to give your worries to God, and let Him take care of them? Why do you want to hang on to them?

May I suggest you ask God to show you the part of your heart that holds your stories of potential hurt and sadness. Ask Him to give you the courage to let go of your unfounded fears and create a peaceful heart. He can do that.

Fear knocked at the door. Faith answered, and lo, no one was there.

Author unknown

Oh, God,

Thank you for caring about my fear. It is so good to know that you really want me to have a peaceful heart. Please help me distinguish between concerns that require me to pay attention to a situation or problem, and fears that are unfounded. Thank you, again, for caring about my story

Amen.

Bad Days

Imagine how you would feel. Someone you have taken long walks with, prayed with, ate fish dinners with, gone boating with, and considered part of your inner circle as a disciple has disappointed you. He abandoned when you needed him, and now, he's going to betray you.

Talk about having a really bad day.

Isn't it hard to imagine Jesus in such a human place? I think of his birth, his teachings, his miracles, but I don't often think of him as a person. Someone who had problems, disappointments, and sadness. Someone who was betrayed by a friend named Judas.

Betrayal by a friend or co-worker is like a slap to the face. So often, we don't see it coming. I wonder why that is.

I recall a particularly challenging leadership situation I faced. The company I worked for had gone through an extremely difficult period. My team was struggling, worrying about their jobs, our company's future, and a significant amount of work still ahead of us. I was working hard at trying to keep the team focused and energized, but in hindsight, I wasn't doing it very well. Then one of my team members filed a union grievance against me. The claim was that I had treated her unfairly.

Now, I realize that most leaders are going to face situations like this, but when it happens to you—or should I say, when it happened to me—I felt just horrible. My feelings were a mixture of embarrassment, frustration, anger, and most of all, a "How can this be happening to me?" I felt betrayed by this co-worker, whom I thought had understood my heart and intentions.

As we worked through the grievance, I spent many hours of the day and sleepless hours of the night reviewing the decisions I'd made, considering what I could have done differently, defending my actions, and eventually, accepting responsibility for where I'd made mistakes, with the recognition of the lessons learned. Then I moved on.

My little work situation doesn't begin to compare to the betrayal Jesus felt at the hands of one of his chosen disciples. But nevertheless, I find comfort knowing that he has experienced some of the emotions I wrestled with.

Each year during the days that lead up to Good Friday, I spend time focusing on Jesus as a human being. Good Friday reminds me of how much He sacrificed...for me, of the depth of his love...for me.

Remember, Jesus understands our deepest, darkest hurts and fears. He's been there. Jesus cares about our loneliness, struggles, and pain. That's why He came to this earth. Jesus gives us the promise of redemption and new beginnings. That's the life-changing message of Easter.

"He was despised and rejected by men, a man of sorrows, and familiar with suffering." (Isaiah 53:3). I find comfort in knowing that Jesus had bad days. I find hope in knowing that Jesus had bad days. I find salvation in knowing that

Jesus had bad days…and did not sin.

"Therefore, since we have a great high priest who has gone through the heavens, Jesus the Son of God, let us hold firmly to the faith we profess. For we do not have a high priest who is unable to sympathize with our weaknesses, but we have one who has been tempted in every way, just as we are – yet was without sin. Let us then approach the throne of grace with confidence, so that we may receive mercy and find grace to help us in our time of need." (Hebrews 4:14-16)

Yes, Jesus understands my every human need because he was human. And He is God.

Remember, it was the Lord's own response to sadness, grief, and temptation that led to a humiliating death and the ultimate vindication on Easter Sunday. Wow.

Oh, Jesus,
Thank you for understanding me. Thank you for your mercy. Thank you for forgiveness. Thank you for your grace that gets me through the hurts and rejections. Thank you for Good Friday. And, thank you for Easter Sunday.
Amen.

Shannell and her team of servant leaders.
Greatness is found in serving.

Greatness Is Found In Serving
By Shannell McMillan

    I recently opened my journal from 2005. Scribbled at the top of a page were the words, "Faith allows me to stretch, humility enables me to stoop." I don't recall if I heard this, read this, or had an epiphany, but the pages that followed were an outline of the mission and foundation of my business model and became a driving ideal in my life.

    Little did I know WHOM I would be serving or HOW great the opportunity. When I created this model, I was the owner of a door and window store and found it very satisfying to take the role of servant leader. *My* customers were my employees, and my focus become one of humility, referring to them by name and not position, and introducing them as my co-workers, instead of my employees. It wasn't a calculated decision but a natural evolution as I grappled daily to find my own definition of success.

    I concluded that, if I had to define success, it would not be independent of the people who worked to help me create it, and those were my co-workers. They were the people

> *Please make me into the person I need to be to do the Dream You have created me to do!*
>
> *Bruce Wilkinson*

on the front lines serving our customers and making a difference in the lives of others by giving of their time, talent, and treasure.

What I did not anticipate was the ripple effect this leadership style would have on my employees and how my philosophy and way of conducting business would flow out through them to our customers and beyond.

> *Our yearning is to dedicate our talents and gifts to some form of good-multiplying enterprise that not only nourishes our soul but feeds others on a daily basis.*
>
> *Laurie Beth Jones*

This model of behaviors evolved into a community, a collaborative culture that opened doors to ministry opportunities outside our four walls. My opportunity was to bring a leadership and personal development program to a continuation high school with a student body of 120 students. Only five students a year were graduating when I began my effort, but in only two years, the graduation rates increased by 300%. Another employee began feeding the homeless once a week through a neighborhood church he did not attend, and still, another, along with her husband, started a ministry to go into the streets to feed the homeless where they lived.

I once heard it said that "you don't have to be great to start something, you have to start something to be great." With all humility, I feel my greatness is found in serving.

Heavenly Father,

let me always look to the model of our Lord and His servant leadership. Remind me of the lives He touched and transformed through His washing of their feet, and calling them to dine, and feeding them when they were hungry, or giving them the Living Water when they were thirsty. Remind me daily, Father, that I am part of his body and have the opportunity, everyday, to be the change the world needs to see. Keep me stretched upward in faith and stooped humbly towards those in need as I remember the tremendous gift of being a servant to Your people.

Amen.

George and Joyce Nornes

We're pilgrims on the journey
Of the narrow road
And those who've gone before us line the way
Cheering on the faithful, encouraging the weary
Their lives a stirring testament to
Gods sustaining grace
Oh may all who come behind us find us faithful.

"Find Us Faithful" by Steve Green

Moving Through the Grief

It had been three months since dad died. The shock of losing him had started to wear off, yet the grief was still dreadful. I felt like I was being swallowed by sadness. The tears were frequent, especially showing up when I was driving early in the morning, or in the evening. Of course, my heart would break all over again after spending time with mom.

Mom had endured some pretty tough times throughout her life, most notably the loss of several children. But, she and dad had experienced those horrible days together. They had prayed together, and experienced the loss together. She had leaned on him. Now that shoulder, that hand to hold, her companion, was gone. So, Julie, Lori, and I were trying to figure out how best to help her get through the experience.

Mom's faith has always been the rock she stands on, the anchor that keeps her steady. Whether the times were good or bad, I have never seen faith lived out so deeply and personally as I have with mom. She *knows* from the depths of her being that God will take care of her. There is never any doubt. Nevertheless, losing dad was still a big adjustment. We all had to learn to live differently.

During these dark months, I learned God speaks to us in different ways. The Psalms became my refuge. I would beg God every morning to give me something that would effectively get me through the day. On many mornings, a particular verse would be exactly the words I needed to keep me grounded. And, on those mornings when the words were silent, I assumed God would keep me upright and strong anyway, because at least I'd *tried* to hear from Him. Dad's former students and my high school classmates sent notes and cards, sharing their memories of this teacher, mentor, and man of God who changed their lives. Their words made us smile and laugh. My girlfriends were God's presents to my heart. Even my clients gave me extra time and grace—something for which I am profoundly grateful. And my husband Steve. There must have been hundreds of times he just sat and cried with me, when the pain in my heart just got to be too much. We were surrounded by blessings.

Yet, with all the comfort, support, and love we experienced, I needed to know that God was going to get us through this ordeal. My prayers had a consistent theme—show me that we will be OK. And, God did. Three times.

One morning during my devotions, I cried myself to sleep, my head on my arms at the kitchen table. As I slept, I dreamed. I saw all of us—dad, mom, Julie, Lori, and me—sitting at a table in the snack bar in a Target store. (I have no idea why we were in Target. I guess God likes to keep His stories interesting.) In my dream, dad had taken a little trip from Heaven to spend some time with us. Although he was very loving towards us and clearly enjoyed visiting with us, he was distant. It was clear that he was no longer *with* us. He had found a new home. Dad wasn't sad. He wasn't lonely. My father was happy in his new place. I found that to be such a relief. *Dad was OK.*

My Dad

A few days later, I was feeling very overwhelmed with mom's needs. Her faith in a loving, faithful God was holding her life together, but there were still decisions and changes that needed to be made that would uproot her from the life she'd known for over 50 years. The most significant? Moving her from Climax to Minneapolis or St. Paul. How could we ever get that done? How would she ever adjust? It just seemed to be too much. Once again, I was sitting at the kitchen table with the box of Kleenex, when God spoke directly to me. I heard Him clearly say, "Be patient. It will be OK." And at that moment, I knew. *Mom would be OK.*

Mom and Dad

God met me a third and final time several days later. I was sitting at, that's right, the kitchen table. I looked out the window and saw a deer standing in the trees behind our house, looking right at me. I stared back and felt dad's reassuring presence. Dad had always loved deer hunting, and I knew God was using the deer to send me a message. This strong, beautiful animal was God's way of letting me know that dad would always be around. He'd be in our hearts, our memories, and in our stories. *We would be OK.*

The pain and the sadness gradually diminished. Mom, my sisters and I didn't cry as frequently. We even started laughing again. And God continued to meet us with the words, comfort, and hope that He alone could give us. *We were OK. And, we still are.*

What do you need to hear from God today? What heart ache needs soothing? What pain needs healing? Ask God to meet you, right where you're at. Watch for his messages. Listen for his voice. He shows up in so many ways.

Here are a few verses that became my touch points in those early days of grief over our loss. Perhaps they will speak to you, too.

"Where can I go from your Spirit? Where can I flee from your presence? If I go up to the heavens, you are there; if I make my bed in the depths, you are there. If I rise on the wings of the dawn, if I settle on the far side of the sea, even there your hand will guide me, your right hand will hold me fast." (Psalms 139:7-10)

"The righteous cry out, and the Lord hears them; he delivers them from all their troubles. The Lord is close to the brokenhearted and saves those who are crushed in spirit. A righteous man may have many troubles, but the Lord delivers him from them all..." (Psalm 34:17-19)

"Have mercy on me, O God, have mercy on me, for in you my soul takes refuge. I will take refuge in the shadow of your wings until the disaster has passed." (Psalm 57:1)

"The Lord is my shepherd, I shall not be in want. He makes me lie down in green pastures, he leads me beside quiet waters, he restores my soul. He guides me in paths of righteousness for his name's sake. Even though I walk through the valley of the shadow of death, I will fear no evil, for you are with me; your rod and your staff, they comfort me. You prepare a table before me in the presence of my enemies. You anoint my head with oil; my cup overflows. Surely goodness and love will follow me all the days of my life, and I will dwell in the house of the Lord forever." (Psalm 23)

Something to think about...

What reassuring messages has God given you? When you close your eyes and see your heartache soothed, what does that picture look like?

Vulnerability

My head was stuffed with "gunk." My tonsils were swollen larger than lemons. A red, scaly rash had begun to form under my watery eyes. Unfortunately, I had a speaking engagement.

Since I didn't want to cancel my appearance, I decided to set aside these physical annoyances and do my very best. (I wonder if this is what the writer of Hebrews had in mind when he wrote, "...*let us throw off everything that hinders and the sin that so easily entangles, and let us run with perseverance the race marked out for us.*" Hebrews 12:1). Well, I set my eyes on Jesus and prayed with great perseverance that I would do a good job.

In this situation, God didn't answer my prayer in the way I had hoped.

I got lost on the way to the event, so I didn't arrive as early as I would have liked. Then, when I got up in front of the audience, I discovered to my dismay that a very important story prop was missing. That particular story—central to my message—would have to be cut. Panic set in as I began speaking and realized I had completely forgotten my outline, the stories, and where I was going with my message. It was a disaster waiting to happen.

I wondered if I should just stop. Could I tell the audience I was sick and needed to sit down to keep the room from spinning? Could I just inform them that I had lost my place in my presentation? Should I confess that I couldn't make sense of my "cheat sheet" outline? (Scary, isn't it? I'm speaking in public while having a very intense conversation with myself.) Today I'm still not certain what I should have done. However, what I did do was to continue speaking, pulling snippets of stories from my memory bank, and patching them together to build a somewhat cohesive message.

My experience with the presentation was much worse for me than for my audience. The wonderful ladies expressed gratitude and appreciation for my words. Yet, their genuine, warm comments were a mere whisper when compared to the very loud, anxious self-talk I was indulging in about my performance. My confidence in my professional speaking skills hit a new and all-time low.

During the next few weeks, I found myself dreading my next speaking event. My passion for this profession was dampened because I didn't think I could cut it anymore. I couldn't identify two skills that would validate my career. Most significantly, I was tremendously worried that my next audience would hate me.

As I've said a few times in this book: when life is tough, sometimes you have to bring in the big guns…your GIRLFRIENDS.

I belong to a Master Mind group along with four friends—Robin, Chere, Chris, and Susan. We meet each month to help each other build better professional speaking businesses. These were the girlfriends who would get me back in the saddle (or back on the stage).

First priority? Get back my confidence. I needed to feel OK standing in front of an audience. I needed to believe that I was good enough. Then, I needed to move away from my performance focus back to concentrating on transformational, relationship-focused speaking. (Please note: in order to do this, I needed to acknowledge that I had messed up my last speech, admit that my self-worth had taken a nose dive, and ask for help. It was very easy to say I'd messed up. The hardest part for me? Asking for help.)

My friends and I created a Speaking Circle, following a model created by Lee Glickstein and described in *Be Heard Now!* Simply put—the speaker stands in front of a small group of friends and accepts unconditional support and positive acceptance. (The speaker can't respond, "Yea, but…!")

So, three weeks after my less-than-ideal presentation, I stood in front of my four friends. The red, scaly, itchy rash under my eyes had moved down my cheeks. One of my eyes was nearly swollen shut. I couldn't have been more uncomfortable than if I were naked. (Well, perhaps that would be a little more uncomfortable—but not much.) My distress with feeling that I didn't measure up was so overwhelming that I couldn't stop the tears, or catch my breath.

My Master Mind Group
Chris Heeter, Chere Bork, Gaye, Robin Getman,
& Susan Zimmerman

As I stood there and took in the positive affirmations of my trusting advisors and friends, I felt a shift in my heart and my head. The heaviness lifted as I accepted their strength and support. Their eyes conveyed the message that they truly loved me, just as I was. With conviction and compassion, they reminded me that I was loveable. I didn't need to prove anything to anyone.

> *The healthy and strong individual is the one who asks for help when he needs it. Whether he's got an abscess on his knee, or in his soul.*
>
> *Rona Barrett*

Basically, the transformation took place because I was willing to be vulnerable. I was willing to say, "I'm a mess. I need help to get back on track." You know, that's exactly where God asks us to be. That's where He meets us. *"But he said to me, 'My grace is sufficient for you, for my power is made perfect in weakness.'"* (2 Corinthians 12:9)

God calls you to himself, just as you are. You do not need to "get your life together," overcome your bad habits, or feel like you are worthy before you respond to His call. If you come to Him as a perfectly-wrapped package, complete with the colored bow, you give Him nothing to work with. You have no need. You will not experience any greater joy or peace or fulfillment than you have at the moment. That's not enough. I guarantee you.

Show up at God's footstool just as you are—in humility, vulnerability, and honesty. Don't pretend that things are better than they really are. Don't for one minute believe that you can get through life on your own. Accept God's forgiveness and His love. Accept His bountiful grace. God's Clearing Circle is always available.

Remember, no one will love you, accept you, and affirm you more deeply than our loving God.

Dear God,
Thank you for your transforming love.
Thank you for wanting to be in a relationship with me, just as I am. Thank you for accepting me...with all my bad habits, annoyances, blunders...and rashes.

Amen.

Phew... Staying fit ain't easy!

Fit, Fun, and Fabulous

I joined a "Get Fit Boot Camp" at my local YMCA. Good grief. What was I thinking?

When I work out on my own, I think I'm doing quite well. How do I know? Because everything hurts. I make certain to thank God for every breath I'm still able to take, and I only go horizontal when the trainer tells me to get on the floor.

However, now there are other Boot Campers to compare myself to. And, let me tell you, I'm not in the running for the "athlete of the year!" I'm gasping for air while others catch their breath. I'm bringing up the rear as others chase their "personal best." Finally, I'm just praying to stay vertical while they casually shake off the tightness in their calves.

Yet, you know, I absolutely love it, even when I'm not keeping up with some of the group. These ladies are fun and motivated—we're all at Boot Camp to get "Fit, Fun, and

> *Don't bother just to be better than your contemporaries or predecessors. Try to be better than yourself.*
>
> William Faulkner

Fabulous," which is our team name. We don't take ourselves too seriously.

This is a great opportunity for me to take myself beyond what I think I can do, push my limits, get healthier, and focus on my progress. I can leave any comparisons to others in the locker room as I encourage my fit, fun, and fabulous teammates. You see, it's not always about being better than everybody else. Sometimes, it's about being my best. (I'm pleased to say that my pant size has decreased as my confidence has increased.) This is SO COOL.

This experience also provides a good lesson to take to the workplace. In our professional lives, we can spend so much time focused on titles, promotions, status, and performance ratings. Everything is measured and ranked. Someone wins, so someone loses. Right?

Now, I have enough business sense to understand the importance of being smart and sharp on the job. Excellence is something good to strive for. It's not wrong to be the best at something. Yet, I've seen too many situations where wanting to be the best required sacrifices that individuals later regretted.

> *God hasn't called me to be successful. Hes called me to be faithful.*
>
> *Mother Teresa*

There will be times when we set our eyes on the gold medal, and we give the race or that chance for promotion everything we've got. That's commendable. However, we also need to choose when we're going to reach for our personal best—rather than contending to be *the* best—to ensure that our life is rich and full of *all* the things that matter most to us.

I'm learning so much about myself in these Friday, 6:00 a.m. Boot Camps—discovering more about my strengths and challenges, experiencing humility and vulnerability, accepting the fact that I'm not going to be the fastest or fittest in the group, (That was a no-brainer!), and I'm celebrating my personal milestones. It ALL feels so good.

Exercising has never come naturally for me. I don't know what it's like to run without my arms flapping and my leg flab jiggling. I always sweat; I never "glisten." But today, I'm feeling fun and fabulous, and even closer to feeling fit.

(Please note: I typed this chapter with my chin. We had Boot Camp yesterday. I think my arms are still attached to my body, but I'm not sure...)

Thank you, Lord,
    For the ability to jump and lunge and lift.
Remind me to never take those activities for granted. And, thank you for helping me laugh at myself. Thank you for the friends that high-five and celebrate exhaustion with me. Thank you for helping me be my best.
                                        Amen.

Father, help me to take off my mask. Help me to slip my hand in Yours and yield the parts of myself I've protected so carefully. Thank You that I don't have to be anyone but who You created me to be. Help me discover who that is.

Nancy Stafford

My Audience of One

"Gaye, you're like a little bird in a cage. The door of the birdcage is open, inviting you to fly, but there's a thin string keeping you tied to your perch."

My friend was graciously pointing out what my heart already knew. Insecurities were getting in the way of my living authentically and intentionally. So much of my energy was spent worrying about being accepted and being good enough. I knew the Gospel messages of God's unconditional love for me, forgiveness, redemption, and faith. And yet, I struggled to get past my own perceived inadequacies.

Measuring up is hard, isn't it? Especially when we aren't sure who is supposed to set the standards, or what those ever-changing standards are. We are constantly bombarded with messages that tell us what to wear, what kind of car to drive, and what social events to attend, just to name a few. Why do we pay attention to these messages? Because we are afraid.

We are afraid that if we don't wear the right clothes, someone will think we have no style. If we don't drive the right car, we won't portray the right image. If we don't attend the right events, we will not have the right connections. And, these are just the easy fears.

We are also afraid of being rejected. Afraid of not being loved. Afraid that we will disappoint. Afraid that we will make someone angry. As our list of fears grows, so does our list of insecurities.

I remember a phone conversation with my mom after breaking up with a boyfriend I'd dated for several years. Actually, it wasn't as much of a conversation as it was a meltdown on my end. My heart was shredded, and I thought, for sure, I would never love anyone again. I couldn't catch my breath and stop sobbing. I tried to speak, but I blubbered instead. "I…dnnnntt…nnnnoo…ifff…I…liiiikkk… staaaaaaakk." My voice carried off into a mourning wail as my hysterics built in a crescendo, reaching a new volume level. Translation? "I don't know if I like steak." It was my way of saying that I had forgotten who I was. I had worked hard to please someone I cared about very much, losing some of myself in the process. I didn't really know who Gaye Nornes was—what I liked to eat, how I wanted to spend my time, or what values really mattered to me. Over the years, I had become an expert in being what people wanted or expected me to be.

> *Am I a prisoner of people's expectations, or liberated by Divine promises?*
>
> *Henri Nouwen*

In the years since then, God has patiently brought me to a new place of self acceptance. Through Sunday sermons, Bible studies, books, conversations, prayer, and watching the faith-filled lives of everyday women, I discovered who I was in Christ—Loved. Redeemed. Accepted. The realization that my worth is based on *who God is*—not who I am—has profoundly changed how I view myself.

In this new place, I'm clear about what matters most in my life. I am easier on myself, recognizing that I have strengths and challenges, endearing qualities and annoying habits, and beauty marks and pimples. They all combine to make me unique. They make me, me. I have let go of much of my need to please and pretend. I have learned that I need to show up and please only My Audience of One. Jesus.

I don't remember when I first heard Jesus called "My Audience of One," but I absolutely love the title. Thinking of Him that way flips a switch in my brain, helping me think differently about perceptions and acceptance. It resets the expectations I have about myself. This gives me permission to be…Gaye (Nornes) Lindfors. What freedom!

"So if the Son sets you free, you will be free indeed." (John 8:36) Yes. I am free to be exactly the person God created me to be. I have the freedom to wake up every morning and exclaim, "Jesus. Today I choose to live my life for YOU…My Audience of One. Show me what pleases you. Show me what honors you. Show me what extends your kingdom. I will joyfully follow your instructions, because it is YOUR opinion that matters most."

Oh, my friends, remember. Trying to be someone you aren't will make you weary, discouraged, and confused. Ask God to show you the person He has called you to be. Ask him to give you the strength and courage to say, "Lord, I want to be me, freely forgiven and confident in your love for me." Set aside the expectations that others have placed on you. Live in obedience to your Audience of One.

Dear Jesus,

Thank you for the freedom that comes in knowing you. Thank you for the freedom that comes from resting in your love and acceptance. Please show me, very clearly, where I am pretending, or trying to be someone different than you want me to be. Give me the courage to set aside the standards that others have set, and focus on your expectations of my life. Thank you, Jesus, for being My Audience of One.

Amen.

Doodle Page...

You've just received an award for being "The Best You."
Write the presenter's script that describes your "Best You."

*Life is not measured
by the number of
breaths we take but by
the moments that take
our breath away.*

Anonymous

Live with Abandon

Imagine three joyful guys making music—Ramsey, Larry, and Leon. Ramsey is better known as Ramsey Lewis, an American jazz composer, pianist, and music legend. Larry Gray, bass player, and Leon Joyce, Jr., drummer, perform with him as the Ramsey Lewis Trio. (If the name isn't familiar to you, perhaps you've heard Lewis' songs, "Hang on Sloopy" or "Wade in the Water.")

Steve and I had second row seats at their concert in Minneapolis a few years ago. The energized performance left me wanting *more*. We clapped, we stomped, we moved in our seats to the rhythm of the music. The room reverberated with noise and delight. It was an emotional event. Simply amazing.

Compare the Ramsey Lewis Trio with the concert I attended a few weeks later. The female soloist had a pretty voice and she looked lovely on stage. She hit every note and didn't forget one word of any song. And yet...something was obviously missing. I don't remember anything about her concert, except how unlike it was from the Ramsey Lewis experience.

What was the difference? I concluded that the soloist didn't want to make a mistake. She cautiously went through the motions, whereas the Ramsey Lewis Trio showed up and engaged in the moment. The trio was determined to

> *You don't get to choose how you're going to die. Or when. You can only decide how you're going to live.*
>
> Joan Baez

have fun and give everything they had to their music and their audience. The audience cheered, whistled, and applauded its appreciation for a Trio that showed up, connected with the moment, and had a blast. And you know, these guys would have put the same amount of energy and joy into their work even if no one else had been in the concert hall. That's what made the experience so awesome, so memorable.

What if we lived our lives with that same abandon, by giving everything we've got into our daily activities? What if we showed up fully present, not wanting to miss out on anything?

It's easy to get into a rut. We go through the motions of living—same routine, same schedule, same activities, etc. The sameness that we create is a safe, easy, and predictable way of moving through life, but is "safe, easy, and predictable" what we really want? Really?

What if there was MORE? More surprises and care-free moments. More challenges, giving us the courage to say, "I can do this!" More risks, bringing us to new and exciting places. More big, deep breaths, reminding us life is a BIG DEAL, and God is even BIGGER.

Christian singer/songwriter, Matthew West, asks us such a powerful question in his song, "The Motions"—"What if I had given everything instead of going through the motions?" What would be your answer?

"...I have come that they may have life, and have it to the full." (John 10:10)

What scares you? What's holding you back? What would you do if you were ten times bolder? God knows your dreams. He knows what you're thinking about. Even more revealing, He knows your heart. Let Him help you move to a place where life is more than just going through the motions. A place of giving it all, with no regrets.

Remember, don't settle for anything less than living life to its fullest through the grace and strength of Jesus. As Matthew West reminds us, "Cause just okay is not enough."

Oh dear Jesus,

Thank you for the gift of life! Thank you for sending me surprises. Thank you for providing me with scenic landscapes, children's giggles, jazzy music, and belly laughs. Thank you for calling me to a life bigger than I can ever imagine. Thank you for walking with me as I live my life fully present.

Amen.

Notes

Writing Your Story

Johnson, Barbara, Cited in *Plan B: Further Thoughts on Faith*, by Anne Lamott, New York: Riverhead Books, 2005, 141.

Kierkegaard, Søren, Cited in *The Life You've Always Wanted*, by John Ortberg, Grand Rapids, MI: Zondervan, 2002, 11.

Lucado, Max, *Traveling Light*, Nashville, TN: W Publishing Group, 2001, 77.

Living and Laughing Out Loud

Kelly, Matthew, *A Call to Joy*, Beacon Publishing, 1999, 3.

Swindoll, Luci, *The Best Devotions of Luci Swindoll*, Grand Rapids, MI: Zondervan, 2001, 92.

My Mind in the Morning

Akers, D. *I Woke Up This Morning (With My Mind Stayed on Jesus)*, Retrieved from http://www.youtube.com/watch?gl=CO &feature=related&hl=es-419&v=wJeVKOTTkHs.

Berg, L. Sandell (Public Domain), *Day by Day and With Each Passing Moment*, Retrieved from http://www.hymnal.net/hymn. php/h/713.

This is My Story. This is My Song.
Crouch, André, *Through It All,* Retrieved from http://www.hymnlyrics.org/newlyrics_t/through_it_all.php.

Walsh, Sheila, *Life is Tough but God is Faithful,* Thomas Nelson, 1999.

Living My Life with Purpose
Jones, Laurie Beth, *The Path: Creating Your Mission Statement for Work and for Life,* New York: Hyperion, 1996, xviii.

Palmer, Parker, *Let Your Life Speak: Listening for the Voice of Vocation,* San Francisco, CA: Jossey-Bass, 2000, 16.

Miss America
Eliot, George, Cited in *Rising to the Call,* by Os Guiness, Nashville, TN: W Publishing Group, 2003, x.

Ortberg, John, *The Me I Want To Be,* Grand Rapids, MI: Zondervan, 2010, 13.

A Time to Sing
Frank, Anne, *Diary of a Young Girl,* Random House, 1993 Reprint.

The Morning Wake-up Call
Camus, Albert, Retrieved from   http://thinkexist.com/quotation/life_is_a_sum_of_all_your_choices/12616.html.

Vaden, Rory, *Take the Stairs,* New York: Penguin Group, 2012, 8.

Girlfriends
Emerson, Ralph Waldo, Cited in *Hearts Touched by Fire*, by Elizabeth Dole, New York: Carroll and Graf Publishers, 2004, 83.

Van Pelt, Lucy, in *Peanuts* by Charles Schulz, Retrieved from http://www.famous-quotes-and-quotations.com/chocolate-quotes.html.

Mistaken
Mandino, Og, *The Greatest Miracle in the World*, Hollywood, FL: Bantam Books, 1975, 101.

Palmer, Parker, *Let Your Life Speak: Listening for the Voice of Vocation*, San Francisco, CA: Jossey-Bass, 2000, 11.

Our Words Matter
Carmichael, Amy, *Calvary Love*, Retrieved from http://www.holytrinitynewrochelle.org/yourti96592.html

Swimming Against the Waves
Ortberg, John, *If You Want to Walk on Water, You've Got to Get Out of the Boat*, Grand Rapids, MI: Zondervan, 2001, 192.

God and My Game of Life
Troccoli, Kathy, *Live Like You Mean It*, Colorado Springs, CO: WaterBrook Press, 2006, 12.

Dry Wells
Johnson, Teri, *Overcoming the Nevers*, Charleston, SC: Advantage, 2011.

I Will Give You Rest
Chapman, Steven Curtis, *His Strength is Perfect*, Retrieved from http://www.metrolyrics.com/his-strength-is-perfect-lyrics-steven-curtis-chapman.html

I'm Lost…Now What?
Omartian, Stormie, *Just Enough LIGHT for the Step I'm On*, Eugene, OR: Harvest House, 1999, 17.

Shabbot
DeMoss, Nancy, *A Place of Quiet Rest*, Wheaton, IL: Tyndale House, 2000, 57.

Vicki's Girls
Crouch, André, Retrieved from http://www.music-lyrics-gospel.com/gospel_music_lyrics/my_tribute_999.asp

Meet My Aunt Idelle
Chandler, Steve, *Reinventing Yourself: How to Become the Person You've Always Wanted to Be*, Franklin Lakes, NJ: The Career Press, 1998, 212.

Troccoli, Kathy, *Live Like You Mean It,* Colorado Springs, CO: WaterBrook Press, 2006, 46.

From Fear to Faith
Lucado, Max, Retrieved from http://www.guideposts.org/inspirational-quotes/12486.

Omartian, Stormie, *Just Enough LIGHT for the Step I'm On*, Eugene, OR: Harvest House, 1999, 148.

Greatness is Found in Serving
Jones, Laurie Beth, *The Path: Creating Your Mission Statement for Work and for Life*, New York: Hyperion, 1996.

Wilkinson, Bruce, *The Dream Giver*, Sisters, OR: Multnomah Publishers, 2003, 191.

Moving Through the Grief
Green, Steve, *Find us Faithful*, Retrieved from http://www.stlyrics.com/songs/s/stevegreen21959/findusfaithful567183.html.

Vulnerability
Barrett, Rona, Cited in *The Book of Positive Quotations*, arr. by John Cook, Minneapolis, MN: Fairview Press, 1997, 87.

Fit, Fun, and Fabulous
Faulkner, William, Cited in *The Book of Positive Quotations*, arr. by John Cook, Minneapolis, MN: Fairview Press, 1997, 334.

Mother Teresa, Cited in *Hearts Touched by Fire*, by Elizabeth Dole, New York: Carroll and Graf Publishers, 2004, 60.

My Audience of One
Nouwen, Henri, Cited in *Beauty by the Book,* by Nancy Stafford, Sisters, OR: Multnomah Press, 2002, 93.

Stafford, Nancy, *Beauty by the Book*, Sisters, OR: Multnomah Press, 2002, 90.

Live with Abandon
Baez, Joan, Cited in *The Book of Positive Quotations*, arr. by John Cook, Minneapolis, MN: Fairview Press, 1997, 311.

West, Matthew, *The Motions*, Retrieved from http://www.lyricstime.com/matthew-west-the-motions-lyrics.html.

Meet the Contributing Authors

Julia Charron

Trying to contain Julia's cheerful personality is harder than capturing sunlight in a glass jar! Julia is 15 years old and lives in Winona, Minnesota. She is a delightful actor to watch in the school plays. She also sings in the show choir and participates in volleyball, basketball, soccer, and track and field.

Julia's favorite Bible verse is 1 John 4:18, "There is no fear in love...perfect love drives out fear." When Julia enters a room, she brings a lot of conversation, fun, and a joyful heart. (She is also Gaye's favorite youngest niece.)

Kelsey Charron

What do you get when you combine a compassionate heart, a witty sense of humor, and a loyal friend? Kelsey Charron! Kelsey is 16 years old and lives in Winona, Minnesota. She is an avid reader and an awesome dance choreographer. She participates in volleyball, basketball, track, school plays, show choir, and serves in leadership roles at school.

Kelsey's favorite Bible verse is Romans 12:1, "Therefore, I urge you, brothers and sisters, in view of God's mercy, to offer your bodies as a living sacrifice, holy and pleasing to

God—this is your true and proper worship." Kelsey has a heart as big as the world—and her humor and empathy fill the space. (She is also Gaye's favorite oldest niece.)

Donna Fagerstrom

Donna is an identical twin, ministry partner and wife to Doug Fagerstrom, mom to cherished daughter Darci (and favorite son-in-love Jay), worship leader, author, conference speaker, and messenger of God's love.

Over the last 30 years, Donna has led worship for "Speak Up with Confidence Seminars," the Annual Coffee Break Conference, and for 20 years at Calvary Church in Grand Rapids, Mich. From 2003-2009, Donna was the "First Lady" providing encouragement and leadership at Grand Rapids Theological Seminary, where her husband was the President. Currently, Donna serves alongside her husband as they travel throughout the USA and other countries to provide leadership and oversight to Converge Worldwide, a national and international church planting and church growth movement

Donna would be quick to say, "There is JOY in serving Jesus and others."

Teri Johnson

Teri Johnson is the President and Founder of Keeping it Personal (www.KeepingItPersonal.com). She is author of the book, *Overcoming the Nevers*, a speaker, and sought-after personal growth expert. Her unique coaching strategies have helped transform the lives of her clients, enlightening, guiding and motivating them to achieve even their most deeply desired goals. Great conversations while sipping coffee, and soaking up as many sunsets as she can, make her tick — along with running and taking pictures. She's passionate about helping others; an encourager and a cheerleader to many.

Teri lives a joy-filled life deeply devoted to her husband, her two boys, and her relationship with God. Connect with Teri at www.terijohnson.com.

Beth Kothe

Beth Kothe has learned life lessons the hard way. She seeks to understand, loves deeply and enjoys working hard to make a difference in this world. After twenty years in the corporate world, she stepped off the carousel to focus on Jesus and her family.

Beth is blessed to be the wife of Dale, mom of Alex and Elise, stepmom of Kate and Chris, and grandma of Kylee Amelia. She loves to write and sing and inspire others to live their lives in grace and peace and joy. You can find her blog, Grace-full Thoughts, at http://ejkothe.wordpress.com/.

Shannell McMillan

Shannell's mission is to inspire, encourage and restore wholeness in herself and others. As Director of the Youth Development Academy at Avalon and Eagle Tree Continuation High Schools, Shannell creates programs to enrich the lives of the disenfranchised communities of Los Angeles.

Shannell formerly served as President and Founder of Alpine Door, Window & Design. Through her business success, her work as a passionate community supporter, and as a leadership consultant and trainer of THE PATH family products for Laurie Beth Jones, Inc., Shannell has influenced the lives of hundreds of future leaders.

Leadership developer. Mentor. Team builder. Philanthropist. Shannell is changing the world one person and one team at a time.

Meet
Stephanie Hofhenke

This book's cover and interior design were created by Stephanie Hofhenke. She is the ideal partner for small business owners and marketing departments who are looking for creative ideas, graphic designs, and website support. She offers her clients a value-added blend of skills and experience. Stephanie can take an idea from the back of a napkin, create a unique, professional marketing plan, and then create the services or pieces required to execute the plan.

Building on her 10+ years of sales and marketing experience in the corporate world, Stephanie started her own company, String Marketing, in 2011. Clients most frequently ask her to work on graphic design projects (print and web), website maintenance, tradeshow booth designs, and the development of marketing plans. The feedback she receives is consistent: Stephanie delivers exceptional work, on time, and on budget, and she is extremely easy to work with.

Stephanie and her husband Tim, and their two children live in Minneapolis, Minnesota.

You can reach Stephanie at Stephanie@StringMarketing.net.

Gaye Lindfors is a business woman, author, and professional speaker. She knows the joy and the challenges that come with trying to be authentic and live a faith-based life in a world that demands so much. Prior to starting her own company, Significant Solutions, Inc., Gaye led a human resources team that supported 12,000 airline employees. She has served as the Chief of Staff to a Christian college president and has worked with a Christian family conference ministry. She has the reputation for being a skilled executive advisor and confidante.

As a little girl watching her dad speak in different churches, Gaye learned how to speak from the heart. As a young adult competing in national speaking contests, she learned how to speak eloquently. As a professional speaker, she delivers engaging messages, from the heart, making her a favorite presenter at Christian women's banquets, retreats, and events.

Gaye is past-president of the National Speakers Association – MN Chapter, and author of *Find a Job: The Little Book for Big Success*. She loves music, books, chocolate, and laughing out loud 'til it hurts. Gaye and her husband Steve live in St. Paul, Minnesota.

Gaye Lindfors

GayeLindfors.com
SignificantSolutionsInc.com
Gaye@SignificantSolutionsInc.com
651-560-5075

Encouraging Stories From the Heart

Participants leave Gaye's presentation as changed people. Encouraged. Inspired. Hopeful.

As a storyteller, a woman who isn't afraid to poke fun at her own mishaps, and an observer of life in the real world, Gaye touches people's hearts and minds. She delivers a Christ-centered message filled with hope, encouragement, and humor.

Gaye helps you discover (or rediscover) how to live an authentic life of faith, fully responsive to God's love and faithfulness. You will celebrate *your* story…because *your* story matters. You will re-define success on your terms, without losing yourself in the process. You will Laugh. Engage. Renew.

You can learn more about Gaye's presentations at www. GayeLindfors.com. Or, email her today to discuss your next event at Gaye@SignificantSolutionsInc.com.

65859832R00112

Made in the USA
Charleston, SC
11 January 2017